I0809875

Enrichment Magazine

IN THIS ISSUE . . .

To the Director

This student folder contains nine study leaflets and the enrichment magazine. Remove the center staple and distribute the leaflets as indicated in the leaders guide. This magazine should be distributed at the first session for use throughout the course.

3558 S. Jefferson Ave., St. Louis, MO 63118-3968

1-800-325-3040 • www.cph.org

Written by Edward A. Engelbrecht

COVER: The prophet Jeremiah lamenting the destruction of Jerusalem. © iStockphoto.com

Graphic design by Christina Ensign

This publication may be available in Braille, in large print, or on cassette tape for the visually impaired. Please allow 8 to 12 weeks for delivery. Write to Lutheran Braille Workers, P.O. Box 5000, Yucaipa, CA 92399; call toll-free 1-800-925-6092; or visit the Web site: www.LBWinc.org.

Manufactured in the United States of America

1 2 3 4 5 6 7 8 9 10 23 22 21 20 19 18 17 16 15 14

I Consecrated You

© iStockphoto.com

The Lord describes Jeremiah's calling as a prophet in three steps. In this article, we will consider the first step and the third step before exploring the second step—the uniqueness of Jeremiah's consecration.

A Three-Step Calling

First, "Before I formed you in the womb I knew you" (1:5). God had Jeremiah in mind for this special calling as His prophet at a momentous hour in the history of Israel and of God's people generally. Jeremiah would speak God's Word at a moment when few people were willing to hear. Like Noah before the flood, and like Elijah who served in the Northern Kingdom of Israel, Jeremiah would be a lonely prophet. Yet, he could take considerable comfort in God's Word to him here: "I knew you." No one knew Israel or its needs better than the Lord; the Lord knew Jeremiah would be the right prophet to speak to those needs. What an affirmation!

The Lord ends Jeremiah 1:5 with a global mission statement: "I appointed you a prophet to the nations." The Hebrew word translated "appointed" here literally means "give." God was giving His prophet Jeremiah not just to Israel or to Judah but to the nations. Oddly, this verb appears at the end of the sentence, literally saying, "A prophet to the nations I appointed you."

Between these two statements, the Lord says, "I consecrated you." When you read the passage in Hebrew, it flows like this: "Before you were born I consecrated you a prophet to the nations I appointed you." It is as though the words "prophet to the nations" should be shared by the verbs "consecrated" and "appointed"—a body-solid statement of who the prophet is, with the verbs like wings lifting him up for this soaring responsibility. The word translated "consecrated" is from the Hebrew word for "holy." God hallowed His prophet for the nations. And this point leads us to still another point in the Lord's statement, explored below.

© iStockphoto.com

Consecrated for War

In three other passages of Jeremiah's prophecy, we encounter the expression "prepare war against" someone or something (Jeremiah 6:4; 22:7; 51:27–28). And—surprise!—the word translated as "prepare" is the same word used for Jeremiah's consecration. Jeremiah is hallowed to harrow the nations like a warrior prepared for battle. He is consecrated for war with God's Word as His weapon and shield.

Passages like this may give us some insight into just what holiness is in the Old Testament. We tend to think of holiness as some quiet, dignified activity. To our minds, holy people sit or stand around in white robes or dark suits doing respectable things. But the Old Testament picture seems markedly different. For example, yet another passage in Jeremiah states this about the wicked: "Pull them out like sheep for the slaughter, and set them apart for the day of slaughter" (12:3). The word translated as "set apart" is once again the Lord's word for Jeremiah's consecration. It seems the word means "to set apart" for a particular purpose, which could be something dignified and sanctimonious or could be all-out war. God set Jeremiah apart from every other leader in Israel at that time. He prepared him for dynamic action, a life-and-death mission to the nations.

Called for Daily Life

What God tells Jeremiah should perhaps shake our understanding of our own callings. God calls each person to serve Him with unique talents and through special tasks. But do you see your day-to-day tasks as a divine mission, a life-or-death action?

Okay, perhaps we should guard against treating our desk jobs like planning an invasion or driving for errands like we are blowing through enemy lines. Blitzing our way through daily life is not what God has in mind. Rather, He wants us to see ourselves as uniquely called and as serving our heavenly commander. In Jeremiah's case, the Lord did indeed say, "See, I have set you this day over nations and over kingdoms, to pluck up and to break down, to destroy and to overthrow, to build and to plant" (Jeremiah 1:10). Remember that God called Jeremiah for a unique moment in history and that his tasks were unique.

We may perhaps hear in God's declaration to Jeremiah an echo of Solomon's wisdom about daily life:

> *For everything there is a season, and a time for every matter under heaven: a time to be born, and a time to die; a time to plant, and a time to pluck up what is planted; a time to kill, and a time to heal; a time to break down, and a time to build up; a time to weep, and a time to laugh; a time to mourn, and a time to dance; a time to cast away stones, and a time to gather stones together; a time to embrace, and a time to refrain from embracing; a time to seek, and a time to lose; a time to keep, and a time to cast away; a time to tear, and a time to sew; a time to keep silence, and a time to speak; a time to love, and a time to hate; a time for war, and a time for peace. (Ecclesiastes 3:1–8)*

God calls us to live consecrated lives in His service, to address the challenges of life with the appropriate response. Even Jeremiah was told "to build and to plant" and not just wage war.

Called in Christ

Our Lord Jesus Christ was likewise uniquely called and even uniquely born of the Virgin Mary, known to the heavenly Father from eternity and prophesied about through Jeremiah and many other prophets. Yet, Jesus spent much of His life in quiet work at Nazareth. Although He was specially consecrated by God, those who knew His family still felt surprise when He eventually enacted God's divine mission in His life. Those quiet years from the time He was twelve to the time He was about thirty should inform our sense of calling just as surely as do His dramatic birth, ministry, death, and resurrection.

In Baptism, the Lord consecrated you for a life of service in His kingdom. Just as Jeremiah was uniquely born for His calling, you are uniquely born again through water and the Spirit to live in quiet service and to rise to the occasion as the Lord leads you. As you study the prophet Jeremiah in the coming weeks, pray about your calling. Think about God's greater purpose in your life while you continue to build and to plant, to serve and obey Him with consecrated intent.

A House Like Shiloh

© Shutterstock, Inc.

A cathedral mind-set convinces us to think of churches as permanent. High stone spires and generations of worshipers can mislead us into assuming that a church will always be there when we need it. But many Christians today are experiencing something else. For example, immigrant churches in the greater Toronto area have mobility, moving to new locations as the costs of rent and permits rise. Even those grand old congregations in venerable parts of the city are learning the impermanence of their futures as flight to the suburbs goes on, despite urban renewal.

Israel first put up the tabernacle at Shiloh in about 1400 BC (Joshua 18:1), and there it stood for around 340 years. But when Eli's sons took the ark into battle and lost it to the Philistines, it appears that something still worse happened, which the writer of the Books of Samuel did not record: Israel lost its long-standing sanctuary. We know about this devastating event from only three passages of Scripture: Psalm 78:60–66; Jeremiah 7:12; and Jeremiah 26:4–9. This article will walk through each passage to draw together a more complete picture of what happened to the tabernacle and what those events meant to the people in Jeremiah's day.

Shiloh Forsaken

Psalm 78 is one of several psalms that remember the history of Israel. The psalm's inscription attributes this psalm to Asaph, one of the leading musicians at the time of David and Solomon. On the whole, this second-longest psalm refers to events from the exodus, the conquest, the time of the judges, and the choice of David as king of Israel. Yet, the psalm also pointedly remembers the failures of "Ephraim." This may mean not just the tribe of Ephraim but more broadly the Northern Kingdom of Israel, which was often called Ephraim because of that tribe's leadership (just as the Southern Kingdom was called "Judah" after its dominant tribe). In any event, the psalmist had issues with Ephraim due to that tribe's unfaithfulness.

Recalling Israel's rebellion (v. 56), sacrifices offered elsewhere than the temple or tabernacle (v. 58), and idolatry (v. 58), Asaph went on to describe a particular example of how God rejected Israel. In verses 60–66, he describes how God punished the people at Shiloh, which was the location for the tabernacle at the time of the judges. A foe used the sword against the people there, set fire to young men, and killed the priests. The devastation resulted in everlasting shame. However, Asaph does not tell us when these events took place or who the foe might have been. Clearly, the events took place before God's choice of David (prior to 1031 BC).

Shiloh Valley, Israel
© Shutterstock, Inc.

Cursed like Shiloh

Jeremiah shows that he knows of these events, mentioning Shiloh during his sermon at the temple gate (Jeremiah 7:12). The way Jeremiah describes Shiloh may indicate that there were still ruins there in his day, more than three hundred years later, since his hearers could go and see evidence of the ruinous events. This would mean that, alongside the Lord's tabernacle, there were buildings whose foundations had survived. Some scholars have taken this to mean that Israel had built a temple before the time of Solomon. But more likely, these ruins would be part of a compound around the tabernacle and homes for the priests or others who stayed there.

At the beginning of the reign of Jehoiakim (ca. 609 BC), Jeremiah also mentioned Shiloh, comparing it to "a curse for all the nations of the earth" (26:6). Jeremiah's hearers understood this to mean that Shiloh was "desolate, without inhabitant" (26:9). Archaeology has confirmed that Shiloh did not remain a significant dwelling place after the time of Judges, which also helps us narrow down what may have happened there. (We know from 1 Kings 14 that a prophet dwelt there, and from Jeremiah 41:5 that some others did as well, though these are the last times Shiloh is mentioned in the Old Testament.) Jeremiah's references to Shiloh served as a warning to the people of Jerusalem that God would forsake that city and even His own temple if they would not listen to Him or walk in His Law.

What Happened at Shiloh?

Given what we know from these few passages and from the history of the tabernacle and temple, it is most likely that the Philistines destroyed Shiloh after they captured the ark of the covenant when Eli served as priest and judge at Shiloh in the region of the tribe of Ephraim. In 1 Samuel 2 and 4, we see a description of how the Lord rejected Eli's leadership and his worthless sons, who wrongfully carried the ark of the covenant to a battle against the Philistines. After the Philistines captured the ark, they may also have raided Shiloh and destroyed the existing tabernacle (cf. Psalm 78:60). At any rate, the ark never returned to Shiloh, which remained a minor community at best. Jeremiah could point to this devastating history and warn the people of Jerusalem that the same was about to happen to them—a prophecy fulfilled when the Babylonians captured Jerusalem and destroyed the temple in 587 BC.

Shiloh as Promise and Peace

In view of Shiloh's history, it is ironic that the name "Shiloh" has also been associated with God's peace and the coming of the Savior. This is because of the wording of the Hebrew text at Genesis 49:10, a prophecy about the tribe of Judah rather than the tribe of Ephraim. The King James Version gives a more literal rendering of the Hebrew:

The sceptre shall not depart from Judah, nor a lawgiver from between his feet, until Shiloh come; and unto him shall the gathering of the people be.

Scholars have struggled over the passage, wondering whether the Hebrew manuscripts might have a variant spelling in them that makes this Hebrew word, likely a word for "tribute," look like the name of the settlement at Shiloh. Early Jewish writers thought that Shiloh might be a name for the coming Messiah, a name that would derive from *shalom*, the Hebrew word for "peace." This association with the promised Messiah who would be born from the tribe of Judah has transformed Shiloh from a name representing curse into a name for blessing! One dare not forget the warning that the prophet Jeremiah intended by referring to Shiloh. Yet one may also joyfully pray, "Shiloh—peace giver—come!" in expectation of our Lord's return.

Lying Prophets

At least four out of ten adults think that it is acceptable to lie sometimes, and the results can shoot even higher when the purpose of the lie is to protect someone's feelings, according to a 2006 Associated Press-Ipsos poll. Similarly, the writer of Psalm 116 complained, "All mankind are liars" (v. 11), which may lead some to conclude that lying might not be so bad if everyone does it.

So, is it always wrong to lie? The simple answer is yes, since God's commandment teaches "You shall not bear false witness" (Exodus 20:16; Deuteronomy 5:20; cf. Zechariah 8:16–17). But because life in a sinful world is never simple, people often come up with excuses to lie. The writings of Jeremiah refer to various forms of lying nearly fifty times—more often than any other book of the Scripture except for the much longer Book of Psalms. This article will explore the prophet's different expressions for lying and God's remedies for this common and damning human fault.

Falsehood

The Hebrew word Jeremiah uses most often for lying is *sheqer*. He uses forms of this word nearly forty times. English translations render the word in a variety of ways, since English has a rich vocabulary for describing lies! Apart from simple references to lying ("deceptive words"; Jeremiah 7:4), *sheqer* is translated as "pretense" (3:10), "delusion" (3:23), falsehood ("swearing falsely"; 5:2), and "deceit" (14:14). In chapters 23, 27, and 29, Jeremiah complains about the lying prophets "filling you with vain hopes" (23:16). These prophets wanted to convince people that there was no need to repent. Everything would be all right, they said, because the Word of God and the temple of God were still in their midst. Normally, such messages about the Word and the temple would be great comfort for God's people—blessings, and the very Gospel of peace. But the Lord shows Jeremiah that judgment was surely coming and the lying prophets were deceiving the people, telling them what they wanted to hear rather than the truth.

The word *sheqer* is also used to describe idols. Jeremiah complains, "Every goldsmith is put to shame by his idols, for his images are false [*sheqer*], and there is no breath in them. They are worthless, a work of delusion" (Jeremiah 10:14b–15a). By worshiping idols, the people are fooling themselves because the idols are simply not real gods.

© Jamie Rogers / iStockphoto.com

Deceit

Jeremiah also uses the word *ramah* and nouns formed from this root to describe deceiving someone (Jeremiah 5:27; 8:5; 9:5, 8; 14:14; 23:26; Lamentations 1:19). The root word may mean to be "slack" or "loose," though that is debated. It describes dealing falsely with someone. For example, in Genesis 27, it describes the way Jacob dresses up and pretends to be his brother Esau in order to steal his brother's blessing (Genesis 27:35).

Another word for deceiving is *nasha'*—infamously appearing for the first time in the Bible to describe the serpent in the Garden of Eden. Eve complains, "The serpent deceived me, and I ate" (Genesis 3:13). According to Jeremiah, it is even possible to deceive or trick oneself (Jeremiah 37:9). He uniquely uses this word to describe God's actions (Jeremiah 4:10). A third term of deceit is *pathah* (Jeremiah 20:7, 10), a word best known for a noun form used repeatedly in Proverbs to describe foolish or simple persons who are easily deceived. Jeremiah also used *pathah* to describe God's actions. We will explore Jeremiah's passages about God and deception further at the end of this article.

Empty Words

In Lamentations 2:14, the prophet tells the daughters of Jerusalem, "Your prophets have seen for you false and deceptive visions; they have not exposed your iniquity to restore your fortunes, but have seen for you oracles that are false and misleading." The word translated "false" is *shawe'*, a unique Hebrew word for lying. Most often, Jeremiah uses this word to describe things that are vain or empty (Jeremiah 2:30; 4:30; 6:29; 18:15; 46:11), a use well known from the commandment "You shall not take the name of the LORD your God in vain" (Exodus 20:7; Deuteronomy 5:11). A similar Hebrew word is used to describe empty and desolate places, which gives us a picture of how this *shawe'* was understood.

Rejecting the Truth

In Jeremiah 5:12, the prophet uses another word for lying, *kachash*. He writes, "They have spoken falsely of the LORD and have said, 'He will do nothing.'" The sense of this word is to deny something, to reject something that is true. Just as the treacherous people in Israel and Judah happily believe the lies of the false prophets, they also deny the truth when it confronts them.

Does God Deceive?

As noted above, twice in Jeremiah's prophecies he sighs about God's actions. He says:

Ah, Lord GOD, surely You have utterly deceived this people and Jerusalem, saying, "It shall be well with you," whereas the sword has reached their very life. (Jeremiah 4:10)

O LORD, You have deceived me, and I was deceived; You are stronger than I, and You have prevailed. I have become a laughingstock all the day; everyone mocks me. (Jeremiah 20:7)

This thought was so troubling to some translators that they attempted to tidy it up by translating the first sentence as a question ("Lord, have You deceived?") or by turning the first sentence into a complaint by the people of Judah.

We should first note that God does not say He lied or deceived. These are emotional complaints from the prophet about his experiences. We should note that the prophecy "It shall be well with you" is something Jeremiah attributes to the false prophets (Jeremiah 23:17). They are the liars throughout his book—not God. Elsewhere, the Scripture plainly teaches, "God is not man, that He should lie" (Numbers 23:19). So what is going on here?

© iStockphoto.com

God allows the false prophets to deceive the people (cf. 2 Kings 18:18–22). Jeremiah complains that he allowed himself to be deceived about what God asked him to do. Perhaps, like great prophets of the past, Jeremiah imagines that people in his day would heed his word and repent. Instead, he learned that no matter how much he preached, this generation was determined to disbelieve and chase after lies.

Truth Be Told

At the beginning of this article, we asked the simple question of whether it is always wrong to lie. The prophet Jeremiah certainly exposes the problems of lying and the way that lying undermines faith and trust. In the very last prophetic book, the Lord says, "As for . . . all liars, their portion will be in the lake that burns with fire and sulfur, which is the second death" (Revelation 21:8). Although liars may justify their words by concluding that they are sparing others pain or by appealing to a higher cause, the fact that the Lord condemns them alongside murderers and idolaters should cause all liars to slap their hands over their mouths. (There is a difference, of course, between lying and choosing to say nothing, as Jesus showed us when He chose to suffer in silence before His accusers; Matthew 26:63; cf. Lamentations 3:28–30.)

Jeremiah suffers for speaking the truth to the nations, even the painful truths about sin and exile for his beloved Judah. Through Jeremiah, the Lord declared:

> *If you return, O Israel, declares the* L*ORD*, *to Me you should return. If you remove your detestable things from My presence, and do not waver, and if you swear, "as the* L*ORD* *lives," in truth, in justice, and in righteousness, then nations shall bless themselves in Him, and in Him shall they glory. (Jeremiah 4:1–2)*

Truth stood at the heart of Jeremiah's message; the new covenant he prophesied would be fulfilled in the One who is "the way, and the truth, and the life" (John 14:6). In Him, we have forgiveness for our lies and for all breeches of trust, and we receive His good Spirit to tame our wild tongues and to lead us in wholesome speech. Ask the Lord for the strength to speak the truth with healing intent and effect, to administer most of all the Gospel of truth for the healing of the nations. That is the way and the life that leads to trust and peace.

THE BATTLES OF MEGIDDO AND CARCHEMISH

When archaeologists dug into the mound of what was ancient Megiddo, they uncovered twenty distinct layers of occupation on the site, showing the permanence and importance of this ancient settlement. The city of Megiddo stood within a pass through the Carmel Mountain range, overlooking the trade routes from the Mediterranean Sea to the southwest, the Valley of Acco to the northwest, and the Valley of Jezreel to the east. The location was a natural hub for travelers and also a natural funnel for armies marching into strategic conflict. Generals wanted to control the pass so they could supply their troops and hold off enemy forces.

In 609 BC, one of Judah's most beloved and faithful rulers drove into the Plain of Megiddo: Josiah, the boy king who restored the temple and the Passover. The biblical accounts focus on Josiah's tragic death, which led to the kingdom's downfall (2 Kings 23:29–30a; 2 Chronicles 35:20–27; Jeremiah 22:10; 46:2). This article will describe the broader setting, drawing on accounts in the Bible and other ancient literature. But most important, it will explain the deeper, spiritual meaning of these events.

Excavated ruins of Meggido, Israel

Megiddo (609 BC)

Before Josiah's reign, the Assyrians captured Megiddo and the Northern Kingdom of Israel. They deported its citizens in 722 BC, and Megiddo became an Assyrian outpost.

In 612 BC, the Medes and Babylonians attacked and took Nineveh. Two years later, they drove the Assyrians out of Harran. Fearing the complete loss of their territory, the Assyrians formed an alliance with the Egyptians. However, as the Assyrian Empire was collapsing, little Judah had an opportunity to expand its territory further northward into the homeland of the northern tribes. Megiddo was one of the cities and regions Josiah reclaimed for the Lord's people. Yet, in 609 BC, Pharaoh Neco II, ruler of much-larger Egypt, challenged Josiah's claim as Egyptian troops moved northward to support their Assyrian allies at Carchemish.

Neco II was the second pharaoh in a new dynasty who aggressively pursued Egyptian interests. The Greek historian Herodotus may refer to this victory of Neco (*Histories* 2.159), claiming that Neco devoted his garments from the battle to Apollo in Miletus. Judah and Syria became vassals to Egypt and had to pay heavy tribute, which further weakened Judah.

Carchemish (605 BC)

Carchemish was a city fortress guarding the main ford across the Euphrates River. For many centuries, it was ruled by Hittites—until the Assyrians captured the city in about 717 BC. After defeating Josiah at Megiddo, Neco II marched to Carchemish and took control of the city. The Egyptians held it until 605 BC, when Nebuchadnezzar II of Babylon defeated the Egyptians in a surprise attack, which became known as the Battle of Carchemish, a major turning point in Near Eastern history, when the Babylonians took over all the Assyrian territory and drove the Egyptians toward their homeland. From this point onward, the Babylonians, the Persians, the Greeks, and the Romans would all invade and occupy Egypt. And the Egyptians never sent forth another great, independent army. Their last pharaoh was Cleopatra VII (d. 30 BC), who was subject to Roman rule.

The Greater Battle

Interpreters of the Bible benefit greatly from understanding the broad history of events such as the battles of Megiddo and Carchemish, as well as their effects upon mighty empires. Understanding the events of the Bible in a merely historical way would miss the point of the prophets entirely! The death of King Josiah at the battle of Megiddo deeply shook the faith of the people of Judah. Their devout king was not supposed to lose. God was supposed to deliver them from the mightier forces, as He had during the exodus, as He had for Hezekiah against the Assyrians, and as He had on numerous other occasions. They wondered what it could mean that Josiah had fallen.

But the Lord had already shown Jeremiah how things would go. Jeremiah became a prophet during Josiah's reign, and he saw that things would not go smoothly for Judah. For example, in Jeremiah 3:6, 7, the Lord tells Jeremiah while Josiah still reigned, "Have you seen what she did, that faithless one, Israel, how she went up on every high hill and under every green tree, and there played the whore? . . . Yet her treacherous sister Judah did not fear, but she too went and played the whore" (see also 25:3; 36:2). In this vivid way, Jeremiah describes idolatry and its destructive effects upon the nations. The Lord was showing Jeremiah that His wrath was gathering despite the reign of good King Josiah (see 2 Kings 23:26–27). This was because the real battle Judah faced was not at Megiddo. It was in their cities, in their homes, in their hearts. They had lost the spiritual battle, and the wrath of God was inevitable because they would not repent.

A Prophetic Death and New Life

The death of Josiah at Megiddo hailed the fall of Judah and the coming exile. Yet, not even Josiah's tragic death could move Judah to repentance and renewal. That remained the task of the exile.

In the New Testament, the death of Christ should speak to us with similar gravity. We should recognize in the death of Jesus just how deeply our sin offends our God. He so determined to address our sins that He did not spare His only begotten Son. Christ's death should rightly serve as a warning to those who fail to repent: God will judge. Yet, at the same time, the death of Jesus Christ and His glorious resurrection prophesy something better for those who do repent and believe. Just as Judah could look back upon the exile and return to see God's mercy and favor, we may look upon the death and resurrection of Jesus to see God's mercy and favor toward us. Christ dies to spare us; He rises to deliver us from death (Romans 8:2). The kingdom, the power, and the glory do not belong to anyone but the Lord, and He reigns over history for our good.

Nearly one third of biblical references to the exile are found in Jeremiah's writings, far more than for any other biblical writer. He is the prophet of the exile who, by divine inspiration, predicted how the exile would happen and how long it would last, and who persistently called Judah to repentance for the reasons the exile would happen. In this article, we will explore the five major exiles Israel and Judah experienced, Jeremiah's warnings about the Babylonian exile, the basis for the exiles in the Law of Moses, and their application for Christians today.

Scattered, Exiled, and Captive

Three words—*scatter*, *exile*, and *captivity*—are used frequently when describing exiles in the Old Testament. Each word refers to the loss of one's property and often to the fact that one became someone else's property! Israelites were not the only people to experience such exile or captivity. In fact, after the people of Israel left the captivity of Egypt, they captured people of Moab and Canaan, making them slaves. That was the common lot of people captured in war.

Today we regard slavery as reprehensible—and we should! But in the ancient world, slavery was regarded as an alternative to killing a defeated people. Ancient people did not have large prisons or refugee camps, such as we read about in the news today. In ancient society, the options were enslavement or death. So, when we read about exile and captivity in the Bible, we need to keep this point in view. Although captivity was a horrible and humiliating experience, it could represent mercy. This is important for understanding God's use of the exiles in the lives of His people.

First Warnings of Exile

Already in Moses' last address to Israel, he warns that God would scatter them among the nations if they did not keep God's covenant:

> *You shall father sons and daughters, but they shall not be yours, for they shall go into captivity. . . . The* Lord *will bring a nation against you from far away, from the end of the earth, swooping down like the eagle, a nation whose language you do not understand. . . . And the* Lord *will scatter you among all peoples, from one end of the earth to the other. . . . And the* Lord *will bring you back in ships to Egypt, a journey that I promised that you should never make again; and there you shall offer yourselves for sale to your enemies as male and female slaves, but there shall be no buyer. (Deuteronomy 28:41, 49, 64, 68)*

In the eighteenth century, critics of the Bible proposed that Moses did not really write the Book of Deuteronomy, because themes like the exile were subjects of the later prophets and not concerns of earlier Israelites. According to this theory, a later prophet composed the Book of Deuteronomy, which was then discovered in the temple during the reign of King Josiah around 633 BC. The king read this book and responded by renewing the spiritual life of the kingdom of Judah.

However, one should note that exile was hardly a new theme in Moses' day. It was, in fact, fresh on the minds of the Israelites who came out of Egypt (notice how Moses refers to Egyptian captivity in Deuteronomy 28:68). Also, the most common Old Testament word for exile, Hebrew *galath*, never occurs in Deuteronomy, whereas it occurs constantly in the writings of Jeremiah, who served as a prophet during the reign of King Josiah when the temple book was discovered. It is likewise common in the writings of Ezekiel, a younger contemporary. It makes more sense to conclude that the Law of Moses, and perhaps especially the Book of Deuteronomy, had renewed impact upon the prophets after all or part of it was rediscovered during Josiah's reign.

© iStockphoto.com

Seven Major Exiles

Although Israelites sometimes became captives during raids by other tribes and nations (e.g., 2 Kings 5:2), the Bible records six major exiles when the Assyrians and Babylonians defeated Israel and Judah. The following chart lists these major exiles and detailed information about them. The last four exiles in this list were of special concern to Jeremiah, who recorded them in the last chapters of his prophecy.

DATES	VICTORS	DEFEATED	EXILES	REFERENCES
734 BC ?	Assyrians under Tiglath-pileser III	King Pekah of Israel and Rezin of Syria	Israelites from Naphtali, Reuben, Gad, and the half-tribe of Manasseh	2 Kings 15:29; 1 Chronicles 5:26
722 BC	Assyrians under Shalmaneser V and Sargon II	King Hoshea; this defeat ended the Northern Kingdom of Israel	Israelites; the Assyrians brought exiles from other conquests and settled them in Samaria	2 Kings 17, which provides theological reasons for exile
605 BC	Babylonians under Nebuchadnezzar	King Jehoiakim of Judah	3,023 Judean nobles, such as Daniel	Daniel 1:1–7; Jeremiah 52:28
597 BC	Babylonians under Nebuchadnezzar	King Jehoiachin	832 Judeans, including King Jehoiachin, family members, and Ezekiel	2 Kings 24:1–16; Jeremiah 52:29
587 BC	Babylonians under Nebuchadnezzar		745 Judeans	2 Kings 24:20–25:21; Jeremiah 39:1–10; 52:30
587 BC	Johanan the son of Kareah	For most of the participants, this was a self-imposed exile.	Various Judeans who were led by Johanan into Egypt	Jeremiah 41–43; 2 Kings 25:22–26
581 BC	Babylonians under Nebuchadnezzar	Gedaliah, the Babylonian-appointed governor of Judah, had been executed	Judeans	2 Kings 25:22–26; Jeremiah 40–44

Learning from the Past

Exile and captivity were dark and distressing days for those who experienced them. Moses, who personally knew the pain of self-imposed exile (Exodus 2:11–15) and who witnessed firsthand the captivity of Israel, expressed this distress fittingly when he wrote, "In the morning you shall say, 'If only it were evening!' and at evening you shall say, 'If only it were morning!' because of the dread that your heart shall feel, and the sights that your eyes shall see" (Deuteronomy 28:67). This is why Jeremiah is sometimes called "the weeping prophet," because he testified darkly to the woes of Judah through prophecies and first-hand descriptions of their exile.

Yet we also must not overlook the fact that exile was a mercy-lined experience, an escape from the still darker shadow of death and the grave. God's people had reason to hope in exile. Their history taught them such hope. For example, the story of Joseph, who was sold into Egypt and imprisoned but then rose to the highest ranks of that nation, must have taught them to look for God's mercy in the midst of their hardship. Likewise, the experience of Israel in Egypt and during the wilderness wanderings must have inspired courage. God had a reputation for turning defeat into victory, exile into homecoming, and captivity into freedom.

The Lord told Jeremiah to prophesy a brighter future for His afflicted people. Jeremiah wrote:

> *These nations shall serve the king of Babylon seventy years. Then after seventy years are completed, I will punish the Chaldeans, for their iniquity, declares the* Lord, *making the land an everlasting waste. (Jeremiah 25:11b–12)*

Although the Babylonians appeared undefeatable, the Lord had already planned their defeat and, with that, the restoration of His people.

Study Guide

COVER: The prophet Jeremiah lamenting the destruction of Jerusalem. © iStockphoto.com

Jeremiah Is Called—and Proclaims Judgment
Jeremiah 1–4

Distribute before session 1 for use in session 1.
Use enrichment magazine pp. 2–4.

Resources for Worship

Use these resources for your daily study at home and at the week's assembly.

Hymn

Son of God, eternal Savior,
Source of life and truth and grace,
Word made flesh, whose birth among us
Hallows all our human race,
You our Head, who, throned in glory,
For Your own will ever plead:
Fill us with Your love and pity,
Heal our wrongs, and help our need.

As You, Lord, have lived for others,
So may we for others live.
Freely have Your gifts been granted;
Freely may Your servants give.
Yours the gold and Yours the silver,
Yours the wealth of land and sea;
We but stewards of Your bounty
Held in solemn trust will be.

Come, O Christ, and reign among us,
King of love and Prince of Peace;
Hush the storm of strife and passion,
Bid its cruel discords cease.
By Your patient years of toiling,
By Your silent hours of pain,
Quench our fevered thirst of pleasure,
Stem our selfish greed of gain.

Son of God, eternal Savior,
Source of life and truth and grace,
Word made flesh, whose birth among us
Hallows all our human race:
By Your praying, by Your willing
That Your people should be one,
Grant, O grant our hope's fruition:
Here on earth Your will be done.

(*LSB* 842)

Prayer

Almighty God, You know we live in the midst of so many dangers that in our frailty we cannot stand upright. Grant strength and protection to support us in all dangers and carry us through all temptations; through Jesus Christ, Your Son, our Lord, who lives and reigns with You and the Holy Spirit, one God, now and forever. Amen. (Collect for Epiphany 4; *PCC*, p. 544)

Digging Deep
My Personal Study for Week 1

Day 1 • Read Jeremiah 1:1–10

1. Using a study Bible or other Bible reference work, find the dates of the reigns of the three kings mentioned by Jeremiah in whose reigns he prophesied.

Josiah

Jehoiakim

Zedekiah

2. a. Verses 4–5 record God's call of Jeremiah. How did God call Jeremiah?

b. How does God call pastors today?

3. After calling Jeremiah, what confidence does God then give the prophet in his vocation (v. 8)?

4. Jeremiah does not make up the words that he is supposed to prophesy—he has a source (vv. 9–10). Why is this fact important?

5. God uses six verbs to describe Jeremiah's proclamation (v. 10). What do these activities say about God, who called Jeremiah?

Day 2 • Read Jeremiah 1:11–19

6. God gives Jeremiah two "object lessons" for comfort and encouragement. What was the first one?

7. The second "object lesson" is easier to understand. What was that one?

8. What was God trying to demonstrate with this "object lesson"?

9. What encouragement did God give Jeremiah in regard to his prophetic work?

10. What are some areas and concerns in which the Church of today must stand its ground, against all attacks, like "an iron pillar," because our civilization does not like its teaching?

The Temple Sermon and Other Discourses

Jeremiah 7–11

Distribute before session 2 for use in session 2.
Use enrichment magazine pp. 5–7.

Resources for Worship

Use these resources for your daily study at home and at the week's assembly.

Hymn

Sing praise to God, the highest good,
The author of creation,
The God of love who understood
Our need for His salvation.
With healing balm our souls He fills
And ev'ry faithless murmur stills:
To God all praise and glory!

What God's almighty pow'r has made,
In mercy He is keeping.
By morning glow or evening shade
His eye is never sleeping.
Within the kingdom of His might
All things are just and good and right:
To God all praise and glory!

We sought the Lord in our distress;
O God, in mercy hear us.
Our Savior saw our helplessness
And came with peace to cheer us.
For this we thank and praise the Lord,
Who is by one and all adored:
To God all praise and glory!

He never shall forsake His flock,
His chosen generation;
He is their refuge and their rock,
Their peace and their salvation.
As with a mother's tender hand,
He leads His own, His chosen band:
To God all praise and glory!

All who confess Christ's holy name,
Give God the praise and glory.
Let all who know His pow'r proclaim
Aloud the wondrous story.
Cast ev'ry idol from its throne,
For God is God, and He alone:
To God all praise and glory!

(*LSB* 819)

Prayer

O Lord, mercifully hear our prayers and having set us free from the bonds of our sins deliver us from every evil; through Jesus Christ, Your Son, our Lord, who lives and reigns with You and the Holy Spirit, one God, now and forever. Amen. (Collect for Epiphany 8; *PCC*, p. 546)

Digging Deep
My Personal Study for Week 2

Day 1 • Read Jeremiah 7:1–28

1. Verses 1–7 begin Jeremiah's Temple Sermon, called that not because it was delivered in the temple, but because it was about the temple. How had the temple, which God commanded to be built and was blessed by Him, become a problem for the people?

2. Worship of "the queen of heaven" (Astarte or Ishtar), an astral deity and goddess of fertility, is a problem for God—such a problem that God asks Jeremiah not to pray for the people. Why does God condemn this worship?

3. How does Jeremiah's teaching about burnt offerings and obedience to God's voice challenge the people's beliefs and practices? (See also Leviticus 7:37–38.)

4. Not everyone will hear God's voice. As God tells Jeremiah about this stark reality, how is the problem with man rather than with God?

Day 2 • Read Jeremiah 7:29–8:22

5. Jeremiah refers to Topheth, or the Valley of the Son of Hinnom, an actual location south of the city of Jerusalem. The Israelites practiced abomination there. Although God says this is something "which I did not command," it was more than the absence of a command, but a command not to practice abomination. What was that command (Leviticus 18:21; 20:2–5)?

6. The phrase "at that time" (8:1) usually refers to an apocalyptic time, one either of the destruction of something or of the final destruction of the world (the Last Day), as well as the time of the appearance of the Messiah. To what time is this section referring?

7. "Why then has this people turned away in perpetual backsliding?" (v. 5). God's people don't compare well with other created beings. What parts of God's creation are listed in this section who do a better job of "listening" to God than do God's people?

8. The problem of falsely proclaiming God's Word is raised in this section (v. 11). Why is falsely proclaiming God's Word so damnable?

9. In verses 18–22, Jeremiah again gives a personal response to the people's lack of attention to God's message and what will happen. What is that response?

Day 3 • Read Jeremiah 9

10. Apostasy affected not only one's relationship with God but also one's relationship with one's neighbor. How was the people's attitude shown in daily life?

Jeremiah's Perpetual Sermon: Repent or You Will Die

Jeremiah 13; 15–18

Distribute before session 3 for use in session 3.
Use enrichment magazine pp. 8–10.

Resources for Worship

Use these resources for your daily study at home and at the week's assembly.

Hymn

Hail, Thou once despisèd Jesus!
Hail, Thou Galilean King!
Thou didst suffer to release us;
Thou didst free salvation bring.
Hail, Thou universal Savior,
Bearer of our sin and shame!
By Thy merit we find favor:
Life is given through Thy name.

Paschal Lamb, by God appointed,
All our sins on Thee were laid;
By almighty love anointed,
Thou hast full atonement made.
All Thy people are forgiven
Through the virtue of Thy blood;
Opened is the gate of heaven,
Reconciled are we with God.

Jesus, hail! Enthroned in glory,
There forever to abide;
All the heav'nly hosts adore Thee,
Seated at Thy Father's side.
There for sinners Thou art pleading;
There Thou dost our place prepare,
Ever for us interceding
Till in glory we appear.

Worship, honor, pow'r, and blessing
Thou art worthy to receive;
Highest praises, without ceasing,
Right it is for us to give.
Help, ye bright angelic spirits,
All your noblest anthems raise;
Help to sing our Savior's merits,
Help to chant Immanuel's praise!

(*LSB* 531)

Prayer

Almighty God, Your Son willingly endured the agony and shame of the cross for our redemption. Grant us courage to take up our cross daily and follow Him wherever He leads; through the same Jesus Christ, our Lord, who lives and reigns with You and the Holy Spirit, one God, now and forever. Amen. (Collect for Proper 17, Series A; *PCC*, p. 567)

Digging Deep
My Personal Study for Week 3

Day 1 • Read Jeremiah 13

1. Although we have used the phrase "object lesson" a few times, in this chapter we meet the first of the object lessons with symbolic actions that God gave Jeremiah.

a. What was that object lesson?

b. What was it to show?

2. God gives another illustration to use in talking to the people. What was that illustration?

3. How does verse 16 compare to Paul's words in 2 Corinthians 6:1–2?

4. a. According to verse 23, how easily can someone who does evil change to doing good?

b. What does this say about the possibility of a person changing his ways?

5. Why are the words "lot" and "portion" ironic in verses 24–25?

Day 2 • Read Jeremiah 15

6. In this lesson, we continue to study prophecies and events in Jeremiah's life that cannot be dated precisely. These proclamations contain his perpetual sermon to the people of Jerusalem and Judah. How do verses 1–4 show the somber consequences of the past?

7. In verses 5–9, God repeats the same judgment in poetry, describing Jerusalem's action. What does this judgment say about God's action toward continuing, unrepentant sin?

8. "I will make you serve your enemies." Jeremiah's constant message provoked nothing but conflict (rather than repentance), leading to Jeremiah's complaint in verse 10. Why is this complaint and God's answer particularly startling? (See Jeremiah 1:5.)

9. In verses 15–21, Jeremiah continues to lament his position in life and asks God for comfort. Although part of the response that God gives Jeremiah sounds like a reprimand, part of it is certainly a means for comfort.

a. What was Jeremiah's complaint here?

b. What was God's response?

10. Jeremiah can be seen as a type of Jesus; that is, his life prefigured in some way that of Jesus. What in Jeremiah's life makes him Christlike?

Life after King Josiah: The Beginning of the End

Jeremiah 20; 23; 26; 25; 36

Distribute before session 4 for use in session 4.
Use enrichment magazine pp. 11–13.

Resources for Worship

Use these resources for your daily study at home and at the week's assembly.

Hymn

Let us ever walk with Jesus,
Follow His example pure,
Through a world that would deceive us
And to sin our spirits lure.
Onward in His footsteps treading,
Pilgrims here, our home above,
Full of faith and hope and love,
Let us do the Father's bidding.
Faithful Lord, with me abide;
I shall follow where You guide.

Let us suffer here with Jesus
And with patience bear our cross.
Joy will follow all our sadness;
Where He is, there is no loss.
Though today we sow no laughter,
We shall reap celestial joy;
All discomforts that annoy
Shall give way to mirth hereafter.
Jesus, here I share Your woe;
Help me there Your joy to know.

Let us gladly die with Jesus.
Since by death He conquered death,
He will free us from destruction,
Give to us immortal breath.
Let us mortify all passion
That would lead us into sin;
And the grave that shuts us in
Shall but prove the gate to heaven.
Jesus, here with You I die,
There to live with You on high.

Let us also live with Jesus.
He has risen from the dead
That to life we may awaken.
Jesus, You are now our head.
We are Your own living members;
Where You live, there we shall be
In Your presence constantly,
Living there with You forever.
Jesus, let me faithful be,
Life eternal grant to me.

(*LSB* 685; text © 1978 *Lutheran Book of Worship*)

Prayer

Almighty God, by the working of Your Holy Spirit, grant that we may gladly hear Your Word proclaimed among us and follow its directing; through Jesus Christ, Your Son, our Lord, who lives and reigns with You and the Holy Spirit, one God, now and forever. Amen. (Collect for Proper 8, Series A; *PCC*, p. 564)

Digging Deep
My Personal Study for Week 4

Day 1 • Read Jeremiah 20

1. Although Jeremiah gives no precise date, the events in the first two chapters this week probably occurred after the death of King Josiah. Jeremiah was persecuted for his proclamation of God's Word. After reading 19:15 and chapter 20, summarize below how Jeremiah was persecuted.

2. a. What was Pashhur's punishment?

b. Why can Jeremiah say that Pashhur "prophesied falsely" (v. 6)?

3. Jeremiah 20:7–13 is paired with Matthew 10:5a, 21–33 as the public reading in some churches during the Sundays after Pentecost (e.g., *LSB* Series A Proper 7). How do these verses of Jeremiah exemplify Jesus' words in the Gospel, especially verse 22: "You will be hated by all for My name's sake. But the one who endures to the end will be saved"?

4. **Challenge question.** As we saw in chapter 15, one can see Christlike elements in these verses (7–13). What are some of the comparisons with Jesus' life? (For a challenge, compare the middle third of verse 7 with Luke 22:41–44.)

Day 2 • Read Jeremiah 23

5. "Shepherds" refers here to the leaders of Judah. What was God's judgment of them and judgment on them?

6. How is the exodus compared to the return from exile in verses 7–8?

7. God compares the prophets of Samaria (the Northern Kingdom of Israel) with the prophets of Jerusalem (the Southern Kingdom of Judah) in verses 13–14. How do the prophets of Judah fare in the comparison?

8. God warns against listening to prophets who speak visions of their own mind, rather than from the mouth of the Lord. How do you determine if a prophet is speaking visions of his own mind?

9. "Who among them has stood in the council of the Lord (v. 18)?" is a rhetorical question. None of the lying prophets have done so. Jesus has stood fully in the council of God. What does that matter for you? (See John 1:1; Matthew 11:27; Hebrews 1:1–2.)

Between the First Deportation and the Fall of the Kingdom of Judah

Jeremiah 21; 29; 27–28; 37; 38

Distribute before session 5 for use in session 5.
Use enrichment magazine pp. 14–17.

Resources for Worship

Use these resources for your daily study at home and at the week's assembly.

Hymn

Lord, keep us steadfast in Your Word;
Curb those who by deceit or sword
Would wrest the kingdom from Your Son
And bring to naught all He has done.

Lord Jesus Christ, Your pow'r make known,
For You are Lord of lords alone;
Defend Your holy Church that we
May sing Your praise eternally.

O Comforter of priceless worth,
Send peace and unity on earth;
Support us in our final strife
And lead us out of death to life.

(*LSB* 655)

Prayer

Merciful Lord, cleanse and defend Your Church by the sacrifice of Christ. United with Him in Holy Baptism, give us grace to receive with thanksgiving the fruits of His redeeming work and daily follow in His way; through the same Jesus Christ, Your Son, our Lord, who lives and reigns with You and the Holy Spirit, one God, now and forever. Amen. (Collect for Proper 15, Series C; *PCC*, p. 586)

Digging Deep
My Personal Study for Week 5

Day 1 • Read Jeremiah 21

1. For the background to a rather quick change of kings, read 2 Kings 23:36–37; 24:1, 8–12, 17 and summarize what is happening among the kings in Judah.

2. Zedekiah started reigning in 597 BC. Read 2 Kings 19:1–4; 24:19 and compare Zedekiah to Hezekiah. What is different about these rulers?

3. What was Jeremiah's response to the king?

4. What was Jeremiah's announcement to the people?

Day 2 • Read Jeremiah 29

5. The letters given in Jeremiah 29 were written between the time of the first deportation in 597 BC and perhaps 595 BC. God gave advice through Jeremiah for the people in exile. Why might this advice have seemed odd to the exiles?

6. What was God's promise to the exiles?

7. Some of the people who had been taken into exile were prophesying among the exiles. What was the problem with that?

8. Another letter came from Babylon, written by Shemaiah to Zephaniah, who was in charge of the temple in Jerusalem. What was Shemaiah's complaint?

9. Jeremiah responded with another letter to the exiles in Babylonia. What were his comments about Shemaiah?

Day 3 • Read Jeremiah 27–28

10. Jeremiah 27:1 sounds like it is written concerning the first year of Zedekiah's reign, but Jeremiah 28:1 clarifies that both chapters were written concerning the fourth year of Zedekiah's reign; that is, 594 BC. Jeremiah asks the people to take action and describes what will happen if they don't do it. How did Jeremiah demonstrate his message?

Consolation for Judah—Promise of a New Covenant

Jeremiah 30–31

Distribute before session 6 for use in session 6.
Use enrichment magazine pp. 18–19, 23–25.

Resources for Worship

Use these resources for your daily study at home and at the week's assembly.

Hymn

Christ Jesus lay in death's strong bands
For our offenses given;
But now at God's right hand He stands
And brings us life from heaven.
Therefore let us joyful be
And sing to God right thankfully
Loud songs of alleluia!
Alleluia!

No son of man could conquer death,
Such ruin sin had wrought us.
No innocence was found on earth,
And therefore death had brought us
Into bondage from of old
And ever grew more strong and bold
And held us as its captive.
Alleluia!

Christ Jesus, God's own Son, came down,
His people to deliver;
Destroying sin, He took the crown
From death's pale brow forever:
Stripped of pow'r, no more it reigns;
An empty form alone remains;
Its sting is lost forever.
Alleluia!

It was a strange and dreadful strife
When life and death contended;
The victory remained with life,
The reign of death was ended.
Holy Scripture plainly saith
That death is swallowed up by death,
Its sting is lost forever.
Alleluia!

Here our true Paschal Lamb we see,
Whom God so freely gave us;
He died on the accursèd tree—
So strong His love—to save us.
See, His blood now marks our door;
Faith points to it; death passes o'er,
And Satan cannot harm us.
Alleluia!

So let us keep the festival
To which the Lord invites us;
Christ is Himself the joy of all,
The sun that warms and lights us.
Now His grace to us imparts
Eternal sunshine to our hearts;
The night of sin is ended.
Alleluia!

Then let us feast this Easter Day
On Christ, the bread of heaven;
The Word of grace has purged away
The old and evil leaven.
Christ alone our souls will feed;
He is our meat and drink indeed;
Faith lives upon no other!
Alleluia!

(*LSB* 458)

Prayer

O God, for our redemption You gave Your only-begotten Son to the death of the cross and by His glorious resurrection delivered us from the power of the enemy. Grant that all our sin may be drowned through daily repentance and that day by day we may arise to live before You in righteousness and purity forever; through Jesus Christ, our Lord, who lives and reigns with You and the Holy Spirit, one God, now and forever. Amen. (Collect for Easter Day; *PCC*, pp. 554–55)

Digging Deep
My Personal Study for Week 6

Day 1 • Read Jeremiah 30:1–11

1. "Days are coming" (v. 3) points forward to a time in history where God will intervene, revealing Himself by His actions. How does God indicate that deliverance is His doing?

2. God refers to the "time of distress" in verse 7. What is God's promise to the people?

3. Who is David their king, to whom Jeremiah refers in verse 9?

4. The "days [that] are coming" will include not only deliverance but also punishment (v. 11). How thorough will that punishment be?

5. God explains why He is punishing the people (v. 11). Why is this explanation so important? (See also Psalm 94:12; 119:67, 75; Hebrews 12:6; Revelation 3:19.)

Day 2 • Read Jeremiah 30:12–24

6. A two-part phrase is repeated twice in close proximity.

a. What is God's response?

b. How does the repetition make the point stick?

7. Another word used twice is "incurable." Why is this a good description of the sin of the people of Judah?

8. "I will restore health to you, and your wounds I will heal" (v. 17). God did this for Judah, but He also does it for us. What was the cost to Him of doing this for us (Isaiah 53:5)?

Consolation for Judah—God Will Restore Judah's Fortunes

Jeremiah 32–33

Distribute before session 7 for use in session 7.
Use enrichment magazine pp. 20–22.

Resources for Worship

Use these resources for your daily study at home and at the week's assembly.

Hymn

Savior of the nations, come,
Virgin's Son, make here Your home!
Marvel now, O heav'n and earth,
That the Lord chose such a birth.

Not by human flesh and blood,
By the Spirit of our God,
Was the Word of God made flesh—
Woman's offspring, pure and fresh.

Here a maid was found with child,
Yet remained a virgin mild.
In her womb this truth was shown:
God was there upon His throne.

Then stepped forth the Lord of all
From His pure and kingly hall;
God of God, yet fully man,
His heroic course began.

God the Father was His source,
Back to God He ran His course.
Into hell His road went down,
Back then to His throne and crown.

For You are the Father's Son
Who in flesh the vict'ry won.
By Your mighty pow'r make whole
All our ills of flesh and soul.

From the manger newborn light
Shines in glory through the night.
Darkness there no more resides;
In this light faith now abides.

Glory to the Father sing,
Glory to the Son, our king,
Glory to the Spirit be
Now and through eternity.

(*LSB* 332)

Prayer

Stir up Your power, O Lord, and come, that by Your protection we may be rescued from the threatening perils of our sins and saved by Your might deliverance; for You live and reign with the Father and the Holy Spirit, one God, now and forever. Amen. (Collect for Advent 1; *PCC*, p. 538)

Digging Deep
My Personal Study for Week 7

Day 1 • Read Jeremiah 32:1–15

1. This seems a particularly bad time for some good news.

a. Where was Jeremiah?

b. What had he done to be there?

2. What did God tell Jeremiah was about to happen?

3. What was the right of redemption (see Leviticus 25:25–31)?

4. What did Jeremiah do with the deed?

5. a. Why did this seem futile?

b. Why was it not futile?

Day 2 • Read Jeremiah 32:16–35

6. In Jeremiah's prayer, he refers to historical events in which God played a role. How does this support his contention that God is omnipotent ("all powerful")?

7. What was the result of Israel's disobedience?

8. What didn't Jeremiah understand?

9. God did not immediately answer the question. What did God first tell Jeremiah?

Day 3 • Read Jeremiah 32:36–44

10. How was the current state of Jerusalem not an indication of the future?

11. God speaks about giving the people one heart and one way and will put the fear of Him into their hearts. How do the words of Ezekiel 11:19–20 (spoken roughly at the same time by Ezekiel in exile in Babylon) help explain these words?

The Aftermath of the Fall of Jerusalem and Judgments against Foreign Nations

Jeremiah 34; 42–44; 46–47; 50

Distribute before session 8 for use in session 8.
Use enrichment magazine pp. 30–32.

Resources for Worship

Use these resources for your daily study at home and at the week's assembly.

Hymn

Songs of thankfulness and praise,
Jesus, Lord, to Thee we raise,
  Manifested by the star
  To the sages from afar,
Branch of royal David's stem
In Thy birth at Bethlehem:
  Anthems be to Thee addressed,
  God in man made manifest.

Manifest at Jordan's stream,
Prophet, Priest, and King supreme;
  And at Cana wedding guest
  In Thy Godhead manifest;
Manifest in pow'r divine,
Changing water into wine;
  Anthems be to Thee addressed,
  God in man made manifest.

Manifest in making whole
Palsied limbs and fainting soul;
  Manifest in valiant fight,
  Quelling all the devil's might;
Manifest in gracious will,
Ever bringing good from ill;
  Anthems be to Thee addressed,
  God in man made manifest.

Sun and moon shall darkened be,
Stars shall fall, the heav'ns shall flee;
  Christ will then like lightning shine,
  All will see His glorious sign;
All will then the trumpet hear,
All will see the Judge appear;
  Thou by all wilt be confessed,
  God in man made manifest.

Grant us grace to see Thee, Lord,
Present in Thy holy Word—
  Grace to imitate Thee now
  And be pure, as pure art Thou;
That we might become like Thee
At Thy great epiphany
  And may praise Thee, ever blest,
  God in man made manifest.

(*LSB* 394)

Prayer

O Lord, graciously hear the prayers of Your people that we who justly suffer the consequence of our sin may be mercifully delivered by Your goodness to the glory of Your name; through Jesus Christ, Your Son, our Lord, who lives and reigns with You and the Holy Spirit, one God, now and forever. Amen. (Collect for Epiphany 6; *PCC*, p. 545)

Digging Deep
My Personal Study for Week 8

Day 1 • Read Jeremiah 34

1. We pick up our readings today from where we left them in lesson 5, just before the fall of Jerusalem. What unenviable job did God give Jeremiah in delivering a message from God to Zedekiah?

2. There was, however, some good news in the message. The outcome was not as bad as one might have imagined. What actually happened? (See Jeremiah 52:10–11.)

3. a. Zedekiah did try to do the right thing. He made a proclamation based on Exodus 21:2 and Deuteronomy 15:12. What was that proclamation?

b. Did the people observe the proclamation?

4. What was ironic in God's declaration of liberty to those who had re-enslaved their fellow Hebrews?

Day 2 • Read Jeremiah 42–43

5. Some of the people who remained in Jerusalem and Judah came to Jeremiah to ask him advice from God. What was their promise?

6. What was God's admonition to the people?

7. So, what did the people do?

8. What did God have Jeremiah do to illustrate that His word would come true?

Day 3 • Read Jeremiah 44

9. What was the problem with the people living in Egypt, according to God?

10. What did the people themselves think was the problem, the cause of their misfortunes?

Mercies New Every Morning

Jeremiah 52; Lamentations 1–3; 5:20–22

Distribute before session 9 for use in session 9.
Use enrichment magazine pp. 27–29.

Resources for Worship

Use these resources for your daily study at home and at the week's assembly.

Hymn

In the very midst of life
Snares of death surround us;
Who shall help us in the strife
Lest the foe confound us?
Thou only, Lord, Thou only!
We mourn that we have greatly erred,
That our sins Thy wrath have stirred.
Holy and righteous God!
Holy and mighty God!
Holy and all-merciful Savior!
Eternal Lord God!
Save us lest we perish
In the bitter pangs of death.
Have mercy, O Lord!

In the midst of death's dark vale
Pow'rs of hell o'ertake us.
Who will help when they assail,
Who secure will make us?
Thou only, Lord, Thou only!
Thy heart is moved with tenderness,
Pities us in our distress.
Holy and righteous God!
Holy and mighty God!
Holy and all-merciful Savior!
Eternal Lord God!
Save us from the terror
Of the fiery pit of hell.
Have mercy, O Lord!

In the midst of utter woe
When our sins oppress us,
Where shall we for refuge go,
Where for grace to bless us?
To Thee, Lord Jesus, only!
Thy precious blood was shed to win
Full atonement for our sin.
Holy and righteous God!
Holy and mighty God!
Holy and all-merciful Savior!
Eternal Lord God!
Lord, preserve and keep us
In the peace that faith can give.
Have mercy, O Lord!

(*LSB* 755;)

Prayer

Heavenly Father, during His earthly ministry Your Son Jesus healed the sick and raised the dead. By the healing medicine of the Word and Sacraments pour into our hearts such love toward You that we may live eternally; through the same Jesus Christ, our Lord, who lives and reigns with You and the Holy Spirit, one God, now and forever. Amen. (Collect for Proper 8, Series B; *PCC*, p. 574)

Digging Deep
My Personal Study for Week 9

Day 1 • Read Jeremiah 52

1. We return to the fall of Jerusalem in 587 BC as a preface to the Book of Lamentations. The king and the army show less-than-stellar leadership when the walls of Jerusalem are breached. What was the result?

2. How did the invading Babylonians destroy the city?

3. Although many people were taken away captive, Nebuchadnezzar left some people.

a. Who were these people?

b. Why were they left?

4. In addition to people, what did Nebuchadnezzar carry off to Babylonia?

5. The chapter ends with a ray of hope. What is that ray of hope?

Day 2 • Read Lamentations 1

6. What is the basic cause of Jeremiah's lamentation?

7. What is particularly troublesome about the sack of Jerusalem (v. 10)?

8. Who is responsible for the desolation of the city (vv. 8, 18)?

9. Who brought the destruction upon Jerusalem (vv. 15, 17)?

10. Although Jerusalem deserved the position where she finds herself, what can Jeremiah say about those who brought it about (vv. 21–22)?

Day 3 • Read Lamentations 2

11. How do the first few verses of this chapter compare to ones like Jeremiah 4:1–4?

12. Why is verse 7 particularly sobering? (See 1 Kings 8:28–29 for the words of Solomon at the dedication of the temple.)

13. Verse 14 is a condemnation of prophets who have seen "false and deceptive visions." What is the problem with such visions?

14. The Lord has carried out His word (v. 17). What is this word? (See Deuteronomy 28:15–68, especially vv. 15, 25–26, 36–37.)

15. Verses 20–22 show how unnatural this destruction of Jerusalem was. How is what happened contrary to nature?

Day 4 • Read Lamentations 3:1–33

16. How does Jeremiah personalize the desolation of the city?

17. In the midst of suffering and apparent abandonment by God comes a wonderful assurance. What is that assurance (vv. 22–23)?

18. Read Genesis 49:18; Psalm 40:1; and Psalm 130:6 to gain an understanding of the word "wait" in verses 25–26. What do these other verses tell you about the waiting that the Christian does?

19. How do verses 28–30 expand upon the idea of waiting and the cross-shaped form of the Christian life that we have investigated?

20. Even though we may experience grief, what is the comfort that God gives (vv. 31–33)?

Day 5 • Read Lamentations 3:34–66; 5:20–22

21. In 3:40–42, we are required to test and examine ourselves. Why would God have not forgiven sins?

22. The ultimate end of Jerusalem and the people of Judah because they did not repent is shown in 3:43–48. What was that end?

23. a. In 3:55–57, when was it that God came near to Jeremiah?

b. What produces such an action?

24. Chapter 3 closes with the expectation that God will recognize the injustice done to His people. What is Jeremiah's expectation of what God will do?

25. What is the final plea (but also assurance) at the end of the Book of Lamentations?

11. There was obviously no compromise between the people and God. How would God show His displeasure of the people's action?

12. What was the sign that God gave to the Judeans living in Egypt that His word would stand?

13. In addition to false worship, what other problem against God's order of creation is shown in verse 15? (See Genesis 3:6; 1 Corinthians 11:3.)

Day 4 • Read Jeremiah 46–47

14. a. What was the first part of God's punishment of Egypt?

b. When was this? (See question 15 of lesson 4.)

15. What was the next stage of God's punishment of Egypt?

16. Why was God bringing punishment upon Egypt?

17. Although judgment is pronounced, it is not total. What is God's promise in 46:26?

18. Judgment is also pronounced upon the Philistines. In contrast to judgment on the Egyptians, what is the outcome of that judgment?

Day 5 • Read Jeremiah 50

19. What do Bel and Merodoch (v. 2) have to do with the downfall of Babylon?

20. Why is God bringing punishment upon Babylon (vv. 17–18, 28)?

21. What does judgment upon Babylonia mean for the people of Judah (vv. 8–9, 18–19, 33–34)?

22. What was the ultimate outcome of God's judgment on Babylon?

12. God promises to make an everlasting covenant with the people, that He would not turn away from doing good to them. What is the sign of this covenant?

13. How do the words in verse 42 reflect the words of God to Jeremiah in 1:10?

14. God finally answers Jeremiah's question in the last few verses of this section. What is God's answer to Jeremiah's question about why God had commanded the field to be bought?

Day 4 • Read Jeremiah 33:1–13

15. a. The Babylonians are the agent and instrument for the destruction of Jerusalem. But who is the cause?

b. Why?

16. Contrast the circumstances Jeremiah describes here with the blessings in Numbers 6:23–27.

17. After verse 5, there is an "about face" in the actions toward Judah and Jerusalem. How will actions toward them change?

18. a. More important than restoration is what God promises in verse 8. What is that?

b. Why is that important?

19. The people returning to Jerusalem and Judah will give thanks to God by saying, "His steadfast love endures forever." How does God show His steadfast love to us?

Day 5 • Read Jeremiah 33:14–26

20. "The days are coming" points to a future fulfillment of this passage. How will the Lord fulfill this prophecy?

21. What is the significance of the phrase "David shall never lack a man to sit on the throne of the house of Israel"?

22. What does God give to His people as an affirmation that He can indeed guarantee that David will always have a son to reign on his throne?

23. Who are "these people" to whom God refers in verse 24?

9. Verses 18–20 are a prophecy about the restoration of Israel. At the same time, it is also a prophecy about the Church, which the people of Israel foreshadow. In what way do these verses apply to the Christian Church?

10. A prince and ruler is mentioned in verse 21 who shall come from the Israelites. Why will he be able to approach God? (Compare what is said about Aaron and his sons in Exodus 28:40–43.)

Day 3 • Read Jeremiah 31:1–14

11. "I have loved you with an everlasting love," God says in verse 3. Yet God also said, "I have stretched out My hand against you and destroyed you" (15:6). Which is the "true" God?

12. What is the significance of "remnant of Israel" in 31:7? (See also Romans 9:6–8, 27–29.)

13. The Lord redeemed Jacob from hands too strong for him. Whose are the hands that are too strong for you, from which God has redeemed you?

14. According to verse 13, God will bring about great change. How will God cause this change?

Day 4 • Read Jeremiah 31:15–30

15. What is the significance of "bring me back that I may be restored"?

16. Does God delight in what He has to do to the people of Judah (v. 20)?

17. Why does Israel need to set up road markers?

18. What did God mean when He said of Judah that He would "restore their fortunes" (v. 23)?

19. How does God's work in verse 28 compare to God's commission to Jeremiah in 1:10?

Day 5 • Read Jeremiah 31:31–40

20. What was the old covenant (v. 32) that God was going to replace with a new covenant? (See Exodus 20:1–3; 24:7–8.)

21. a. What is the new covenant?

b. Who is the mediator of the new covenant? (See Hebrews 8:6–12; Luke 22:20.)

22. In verse 37, God reassures His people Israel that He cannot cast them off. Is such assurance diminished in any way today?

23. Jeremiah 31:40 does not apply to Jerusalem in Jeremiah's day. Compare 31:40 with Luke 21:5–6. To what does the passage apply?

11. Jeremiah was clearly not the only prophet prophesying at this time. There was a "marketplace of ideas" in Jerusalem. There were others who were advocating resistance to the king of Babylon. What was Jeremiah's advice about these people?

12. How do pastors give similar advice to their congregations today?

13. There were also false prophets at the time, and Jeremiah describes one of them. How did this false prophet demonstrate his prophecy?

14. How did Jeremiah and the Lord respond to the false prophet?

Day 4 • Read Jeremiah 37

15. Today we read about events that occurred just before the fall of the kingdom of Judah in 587 BC. The events of Jeremiah 37 occurred in 588 BC. What political event had appeared to change the situation in Jerusalem?

16. What did Jeremiah say about this apparent change in the political situation for Judah?

17. a. When Jeremiah tried to leave the city, he was accused by the people there. Why?

b. Why would their accusation appear true (see 21:9)?

18. a. What was Jeremiah's response?

b. What did his accusers do?

19. a. Jeremiah made a request of King Zedekiah. How did Jeremiah back up the plea?

b. Why did he make the plea (see especially v. 16)?

20. How did Jeremiah remind Zedekiah that both he and the false prophets were in the wrong?

Day 5 • Read Jeremiah 38

21. Jeremiah's life was still in peril.

a. What was the accusation against him by Shephatiah and others?

b. What did they do?

22. What did Ebed-melech the Ethiopian do to rescue Jeremiah?

23. How does King Zedekiah appear in this story? (Compare v. 5 with v. 10.)

24. Even at this late date, God is gracious to Zedekiah. Jeremiah tells Zedekiah something could keep the city from being destroyed. What will guarantee its destruction?

25. Zedekiah again shows his lack of strength as king. What did he say to Jeremiah to show this?

Day 3 • Read Jeremiah 26

10. Our readings starting today can be dated because Jeremiah tells us who was reigning at the time. The events of chapter 26 take place in 609 BC. Jeremiah refers to Shiloh. What happened at Shiloh? (See 1 Samuel 4:3–4, 10–11; Jeremiah 7:14.)

11. What happened to Jeremiah when he preached that the temple would become a heap of stones and the city of Jerusalem desolate?

12. What was Jeremiah's defense?

13. How did the officials react to Jeremiah's defense?

14. How did Jeremiah's situation contrast with that of Shemaiah?

Day 4 • Read Jeremiah 25

15. a. We can readily date this chapter because of the reference to the fourth year of Jehoiakim, which places Jeremiah's prophesy here at 605 BC. How long has Jeremiah been preaching?

b. What has been the result?

16. Because of the reaction of the people (or better, lack of action by the people), God was going to bring someone against Jerusalem. Why would this news be particularly disturbing at this time (see Jeremiah 46:2)?

17. Not only would the invader destroy the land, but he would also take away people in captivity to serve him.

a. How long would this exile last?

b. What would be the outcome at the end of that period?

18. Jeremiah is to give the cup of the Lord's wrath not only to Judah and Jerusalem, but also to all the surrounding nations. What was the cup of God's wrath?

19. God also offers a cup of blessing. Describe it below. (See 1 Corinthians 10:16 for help.)

Day 5 • Read Jeremiah 36

20. God asked Jeremiah to prepare a scroll of everything that He had asked Jeremiah to speak against Judah and Israel and the nations. Why was this?

21. Who read the scroll for Jeremiah in the temple?

22. What was the response of the people and the officials?

23. What was the king's response?

24. How do leaders today respond to God's Word in similar ways?

Day 3 • Read Jeremiah 16

11. God told Jeremiah that he was to live his life in such a way that his own life would be a foreshadowing of what was to come.

a. What was Jeremiah not to do (vv. 1–4)?

b. How did that foreshadow the future?

12. Jeremiah was to refrain from other activities (vv. 5–9). How did that foreshadow the future for Judah?

13. Jeremiah's lifestyle (and words) were meant to encourage a response.

a. What was his hearers' question?

b. What was Jeremiah's response?

14. a. Christians are also to live their lives to encourage a response from others. How should they live their lives?

b. What is the response to inquirers (1 Peter 3:15)?

15. Everything might seem like doom and gloom in Jeremiah, but there are occasional glimpses of light. We have one of those glimpses here in chapter 16. What is that glimpse of hope?

Day 4 • Read Jeremiah 17

16. The reason for God's judgment against the children of Israel was evident from their actions, which were self-condemnatory. What was God's response to this?

17. Verses 5–8 contrast the man who is cursed and the man who is blessed. Psalm 1 also uses the analogy of a tree planted by water.

a. In the psalm, who is like a tree planted by water?

b. How does that expand upon Jeremiah 17:8?

18. God declares, "I the Lord search the heart." What does He find there (Romans 7:18–20; Psalm 51:10)?

19. Jeremiah's emphasis in verse 22 on not carrying a burden on the Sabbath was appropriate for his day. His purpose, however, was not to spell out new (or old, as the case is) laws; rather, he had a reason to underscore this. We are no longer under the Law, but under grace; how do we keep the Sabbath Day holy?

20. God promised Jeremiah that if the people kept the Sabbath Day holy, then Jerusalem would be inhabited forever. Has He kept His promise? (See Hebrews 4:9–10 and also the hymn "Oh, What Their Joy" [*LSB* 675:1].)

Day 5 • Read Jeremiah 18

21. God gives Jeremiah another(!) object lesson in the opening verses of chapter 18. What did Jeremiah observe?

22. What was Jeremiah to learn from this observation?

23. God would relent of punishing a nation if that nation repented. What is a famous example of God actually doing this (see Jonah 3:10)?

24. In which of the two categories did the kingdom of Judah fit?

25. Why were the people of Judah stuck in their pattern (v. 18)?

11. "Shall I not punish them for these things?" asks God (v. 9). What is God's answer to His own question?

12. Why does Jeremiah call for the mourning women to come?

13. Boasting can be okay, as long as the object is correct.

a. What are examples of incorrect boasting?

b. What are examples of correct boasting?

Day 4 • Read Jeremiah 10

14. What is Jeremiah's argument about the futility of worshiping idols?

15. How does Jeremiah describe the true God in contrast with idols?

16. God established the world by His wisdom (v. 12). Who or what is God's wisdom (see Proverbs 3:19; 8:12, 22–26; John 1:1–3)?

17. Although "Israel is the tribe of His inheritance," what is God doing to Israel?

18. Who gets the blame for the people not knowing what is right?

Day 5 • Read Jeremiah 11

19. a. God returns to the seminal covenant He made with His people when He brought them out of Egypt, so that He would be their God and they would be His people. What was the commitment of the people in this covenant?

b. What was God's commitment?

20. God carried out His part of the covenant. The people did not. What was the penalty for the people?

21. What is the tragic irony of this disaster (v. 17)?

22. a. It may be difficult in verses 18–20 to see what is happening, because the antecedents of the personal pronouns are not given. These verses are a revelation to Jeremiah that his own townspeople are conspiring against him (see v. 21). Why do they want to kill Jeremiah?

b. What is the significance of "Your vengeance" in verse 20?

23. What was God's vengeance upon the men of Anathoth?

Day 3 • Read Jeremiah 2

11. What did God do to show His commitment to His people Israel (found in several verses throughout the chapter)?

12. "What wrong did your fathers find in Me, that they went far from Me?" God asks in verse 4. There was no wrong in God, yet the people went far from Him. What are the various ways that Jeremiah expresses this "going far from God"?

13. God accuses the Israelites of exchanging their glory for that which does not profit.

a. What is their glory (Exodus 24:16)?

b. Where did the Israelites find it (Exodus 40:34–35; cf. Luke 2:29–30, 32)?

14. God's purpose in striking the Israelites because of their faults is not because He is petty, a control freak, or sadistic (for other adjectives, see Richard Dawkins's book *The God Delusion*). What is His reason for doing this (v. 30)?

Day 4 • Read Jeremiah 3

15. Jeremiah picks up a theme he had first mentioned in 2:20 and continues proclaiming it: that Judah has become a whore by worshiping other gods. Look at the First Commandment in Exodus 20:3 and what God says in Isaiah 54:5–6 to explain why this is an appropriate description.

16. In verses 6–10, God refers to the Northern Kingdom, Israel, and the Southern Kingdom, Judah. What lesson was it that the Southern Kingdom had not learned?

17. Jeremiah is not incessant in scolding and chiding. In this chapter, we see the important word *return* appear. God wants His people to come back. In verse 14, God bids them return because He is their "master" (the word used can mean "master," "husband," or "Lord"). That word is *baal*, the same word used for the Canaanite god. How have the deeds of the people turned their relationship with God on its head?

18. "Shepherds" in verse 15 refers to the leaders of Judah.

a. What was God going to do?

b. Why did He need to do it?

19. a. Where is the salvation of Israel?

b. Why does it need to be there (vv. 21–25)?

Day 5 • Read Jeremiah 4

20. God's gracious invitation to a people dying in their sin remains. Being a member of God's people is not simply a matter of outward ritual, but a matter of the heart. Compare verse 4 with Romans 2:25–29.

21. We hear in the fourth chapter of Jeremiah for the first time the specific consequence of Judah's unfaithfulness to God: a disaster that would come from the north (v. 6). Find Judah on a map and explain why this makes sense. Who is responsible for this disaster coming to Judah?

22. Although you named one person as responsible for the disaster in the last question, ultimately, who is responsible (v. 18)?

23. Although Jeremiah is declaring this message of disaster, he cannot stand by and simply make a clinical presentation of the facts of coming judgment. How does he respond to this message (vv. 18–21)?

24. Desolation seems to be inevitable ("I have not relented, nor will I turn back"; v. 28) and complete ("there was no man, . . . the fruitful land was a desert"; vv. 25, 26), yet there is a glimmer of hope here. Where is the hope?

A Future and a Hope for You

In the accounts of Joseph, Moses, and Jeremiah, we may find comfort and determination today. Although we face dark and difficult days, we should not conclude that the Lord has utterly forsaken us. As Jeremiah understood, the Lord is a God of mercy, a Savior, and not simply a harsh judge. As the first exiles of Jerusalem marched north and east away into the Babylonian Captivity, the Lord planned to set the feet of their grandchildren on the pathway home. God would punish, but He would also restore. In exile, He would even prosper them. In fact, ironically, when the time came to return to Jerusalem, many Judeans decided to stay in Babylon, which became one of the most important centers of Judaism in the centuries to come and a home to early Christians too. Exile was for Israel not an end but a means to an end. God spared their lives so that He might prosper them.

As disaster strikes, respond with repentant and humble hearts. Look for God's mercy in the midst of wrath. Offer Him thanks for your Savior, Jesus, and raise to Him your prayers for deliverance, the future, and hope. For He prophesied through Jeremiah:

> *When seventy years are completed for Babylon, I will visit you, and I will fulfill to you My promise and bring you back to this place. For I know the plans I have for you, declares the* LORD*, plans for welfare and not for evil, to give you a future and a hope. (Jeremiah 29:10–11)*

The Storm of the Lord

A feature of Jeremiah's writing style is repetition. For example, he repeats the expression "Thus says the LORD" 151 times and "Declares the LORD" 173 times. But in other cases, Jeremiah repeats much larger passages with different applications. This article will look at one example: the storm of the Lord.

The Tempest

Jeremiah 23:19–20 and 30:23–24 use almost exactly the same words but speak to different audiences. In the first passage, Jeremiah announces God's coming wrath upon the lying prophets. For many readers, the word "storm" automatically brings to mind a thunderstorm. But in the more arid climes of Israel, other storms were just as common.

The Hebrew word for "storm" in this case describes a torrid wind storm. Ezekiel uses this word to describe the winds of a thunderstorm (Ezekiel 1:4; 13:11–13). But Jeremiah, like the prophet Job, refers to the whirling of the wind, a motion that makes us think of a tornado (Job 38:1; 40:6). When it bursts upon the heads of the wicked, it does not do so by dropping rain but by slamming them forcefully. The word translated "wrath" in both passages from Jeremiah is also a term for heat, which may imply that these are dry, angry, withering winds (cf. Jonah 4:8).

Jeremiah's warnings to the false prophets in chapter 23 were focused on 587 BC. The lying prophets would be proven wrong when the Babylonians breached and took the city of Jerusalem. In contrast, the storm in chapter 30 is a distant storm, a storm that concerns those who live "in the latter days" (30:24). Thanks be to God the message of 30:23–24 does not end with a mere pronouncement of wrath but extends into the next chapter, proclaiming the deliverance of Israel, proclaiming our deliverance, for we will survive God's day of wrath like the remnant that returned from exile.

BUY MY FIELD AT ANATHOTH

In 2013, Chairman Barry Diller of InterActivCorp declared he made a mistake when he bought the once-popular magazine *Newsweek*. After acquiring the business, Diller concluded that the new reality of instant news on the internet made a news magazine undesirable to advertisers. In other words, Diller experienced what is known as "buyer's remorse," when getting a closer look at your new purchase brings only grief.

Buyer's remorse was known to Jeremiah, too, after he weighed out silver and signed the deed to his family's ancestral property. To understand Jeremiah's hometown of Anathoth takes some broader reading in biblical history. This article will review that history and help explain why the prophet experienced such severe buyer's remorse.

Background

When Joshua led the people of Israel in dividing up the Promised Land, the Levites received a number of cities and pastures among the twelve tribes of Israel. One of those cities was Anathoth, in the tribal region of Benjamin. The city was likely named for the Canaanite goddess Anat, who was worshiped as a goddess of war and as the sister/wife to their chief god, Baal. Ironically, the Levites who settled at Anathoth did not succeed in ridding the town of this idolatrous name! In fact, during the fourteenth century BC, the region of Benjamin became notorious for wickedness (Judges 19:22–30). If the Levities at Anathoth were not a part in such sins, they were at least ineffective in leading the people of Benjamin in the way of the Lord.

© Shutterstock, Inc.

Around 1010 BC, Saul, Israel's first king and a Benjaminite, was suspicious of the priests in the neighboring town of Nob because they supported David, a Judean (1 Samuel 22:6–23). Although Saul sent soldiers to Nob to slay all the priests, one of them escaped. His name was Abiathar, who loyally supported David and, after David's death, sought to promote David's son Adonijah as king. But around 970 BC, God and the people chose Solomon instead, and Solomon banished Abiathar to Anathoth. It is from this complex background that we receive the prophet Jeremiah, a descendant of the priest Abiathar whose family was exiled from Jerusalem. That made Jeremiah a born outsider in the kingdom of Judah, a priest with no temple where he could serve, someone naturally despised by the leaders in Jerusalem.

A Bad Deal

It was bad enough that Anathoth had a reputation for bad dealing and banishment. But the Jerusalem insider Isaiah hints at yet another reason the city might be despised. In 701 BC, when the Assyrians approached and besieged Jerusalem, they likely cut down the trees of Anathoth to build their siege engines and other war materials (Isaiah 10:28–34). If all the trees were removed, the city would lose all its fruit trees, which take many years to grow back—an economic and ecological disaster.

What is more, in 587 BC, when Jeremiah's cousin Hanamel came to ask him to purchase the ancestral property at Anathoth, the Babylonians were already occupying it! Hanamel was making a ridiculous request, like asking someone to buy property at Paris in 1940 while goose-stepping German troops were marching through it. Only a fool would weigh out silver for Anathoth. Yet, God in His wisdom compelled Jeremiah to do just that—buy second-rate property buried in Babylonian sandals.

Action Prophecy

As Jeremiah explains, his purchase of the ancestral property at Anathoth was a prophetic act. Jeremiah was known for this sort of action prophecy. For example, the Lord elsewhere told Jeremiah to use a ruined loincloth (13:1–11), pottery (18:1–10), a broken flask (19:1–13), and figs (ch. 24) to illustrate prophetic truths. As an unmarried man (16:1–4), he had the disposable income for this type of wildly risky investment, which is perhaps why Hanamel sought him out.

Redemption

Another probable reason why Hanamel came to Jeremiah was that, as a family member, he had "the right of redemption" (Jeremiah 32:6) to act as a kinsman-redeemer, to ensure that the property would remain in the family. This was both a burden and an honor (cf. the role of Boaz in the story of Ruth). In Jeremiah's case, it was nearly entirely a burden; his imprisonment, the presence of the Babylonians, the lack of an heir, and the cost itself were all reasons for Jeremiah to decline. After the purchase, he broke into genuine remorse (32:16–25).

The Lord used this occasion and illustration to show the people of Jerusalem that Judah had a future after the Babylonians would withdraw. Jeremiah's foolhardy purchase was actually an act of deep and abiding faith in the face of trouble and change. The Lord told Jeremiah:

> *[Jerusalem] is given into the hand of the king of Babylon. . . . Behold, I will gather them from all the countries to which I drove them in My anger and My wrath and in great indignation. I will bring them back to this place, and I will make them dwell in safety. And they shall be My people, and I will be their God. I will give them one heart and one way, that they may fear Me forever, for their own good and the good of their children after them. I will make with them an everlasting covenant, that I will not turn away from doing good to them. (Jeremiah 32:36–40)*

Jeremiah never did get the opportunity to enjoy his property at Anathoth. When he would have visited there, he was again imprisoned (37:11–14), and he ultimately died in Egypt, far from home. Yet his prophecy of Anathoth came true! The people of Judah did return seventy years later and settled in Anathoth (Nehemiah 10:19), among other places. During his life, Jeremiah was little appreciated. But as the prophet of the return from exile, he was widely appreciated by later generations (see "Popular Jeremiah," pp. 23–26).

The New Covenant

Today, our intention to serve the Lord may seem foolish to many, a waste of time, money, and even reputation. Yet the Lord calls us to faithfully testify about His will and His plans. We have the honor of making Him known, even in a cynical age. The new covenant that Jeremiah prophesied became our New Testament in Jesus Christ. Through the Word of Christ and the benefits of receiving His body and blood, we are equipped by Him to proclaim His kingdom.

Popular Jeremiah

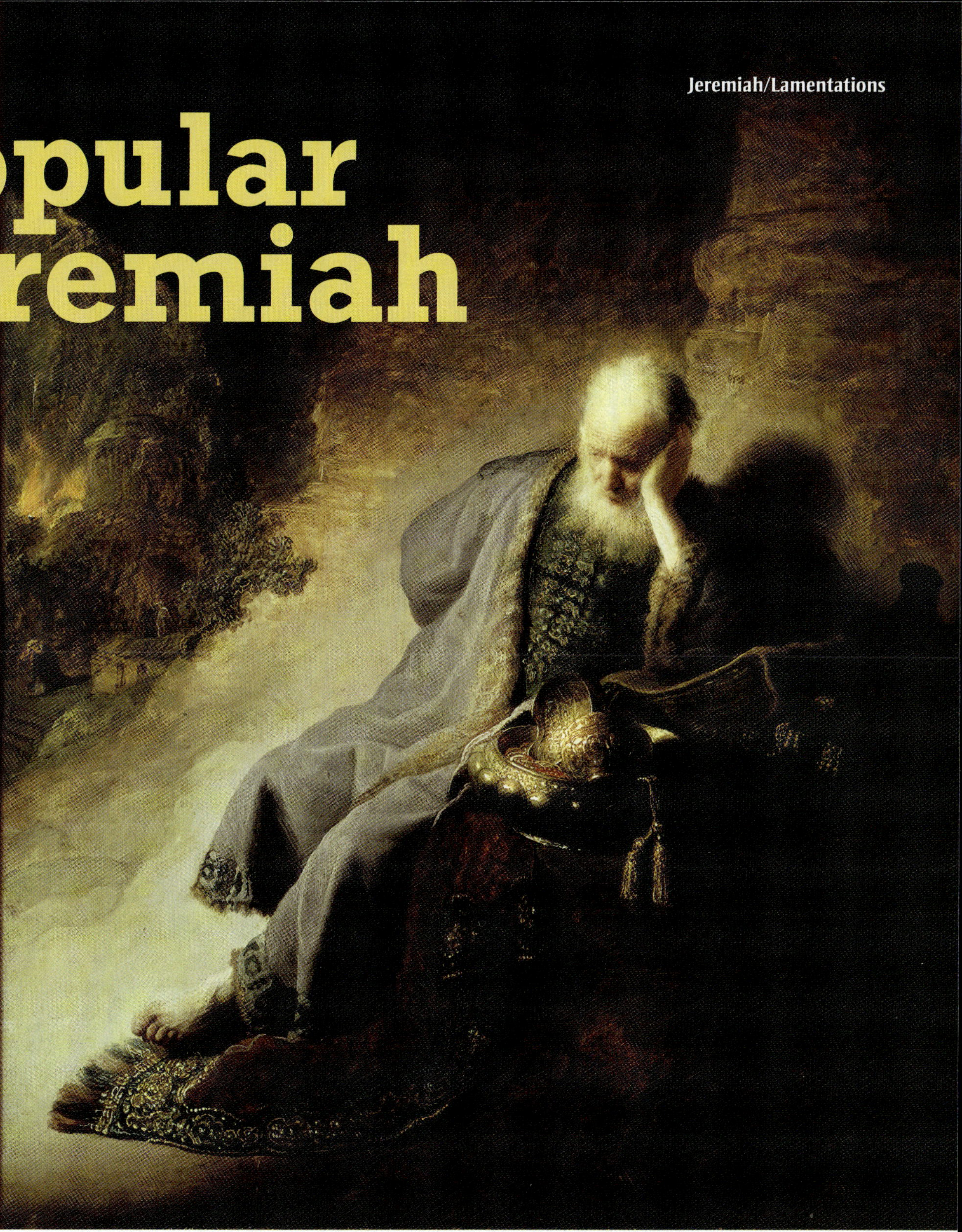

Prophet Jeremiah Lamenting the Destruction of Jerusalem, Rembrandt SuperStock / SuperStock

For many modern readers, Jeremiah stands in the shadow of the gifted poet and theologian Isaiah, whose writings were cited most often in the New Testament. Isaiah's writings also appeal more to modern readers, who want a hopeful message in contrast to Jeremiah's lamentation. Yet, history shows that Jeremiah was one of the more popular prophets and that he gained attention that he lacked in his own lifetime.

This article will survey the ongoing interest and popularity of Jeremiah from Old Testament times into early Judaism and early Christianity. It highlights important and enduring features of the prophet's message.

The Prophet of Return

Daniel, in the generation after Jeremiah, recognized the stunning promise that the Lord announced through His suffering prophet, Jeremiah. In Daniel 9, the prophet describes how he came upon the words of Jeremiah stating that the Lord would end the desolations of Jerusalem after seventy years. Daniel might have dismissed this prophecy in the face of Babylonian might. He might have wondered, "How could the Lord possibly fulfill this?" Instead, Daniel turned his face to Lord in repentance and prayer, trusting that the Lord would accomplish what He said.

Soon, Cyrus the Persian conquered the Babylonians and decreed that the Judeans would be allowed to return to their homeland and rebuild the temple. Ezra opens his book with this fulfillment of Jeremiah's prophecy (Ezra 1:1); the writer of Chronicles ends his history of Israel by citing Jeremiah (2 Chronicles 36:20–23). These writers illustrate the important place Jeremiah had in their lives. He was not just a lamenting prophet but the prophet of return, God's chosen instrument for leading Israel home from sin and exile to the Promised Land and the rebuilding of the temple. Although his prophecies may feel like darkness and hopelessness to the modern mind, Jeremiah was the prophet of hope for the generations that followed him, dramatic proof of God's continued favor toward His people.

Noteworthy interest in Jeremiah is further illustrated by a problem scribes discovered as they studied his prophecies. The Septuagint (Greek translation) of Jeremiah is roughly one-eighth shorter than the traditional Hebrew text, and the Greek text is likewise arranged differently. Although scholars are not entirely sure why this shorter version of Jeremiah was prepared and arranged, it is possible that it represents an editor's attempt to make a favorite prophet easier to read.

The Time between the Testaments

The calling and work of Jeremiah and his colleague Baruch likewise inspired other writers during the time between the Old and New Testaments. For example, the apocryphal books of this era include a five-chapter work attributed to Baruch, which describes Judah's sorrows over sin and the bitter experiences of exile, as well as prayers of repentance and hope. There is also a letter attributed to Jeremiah, written in a colorful, mocking style. Jeremiah supposedly addressed this letter to the Judeans exiled in Babylon and poked fun at the silence, appearance, and powerlessness of idols. It is very unlikely that Baruch and Jeremiah actually wrote these works, but they do illustrate the popular interest in Jeremiah and even attribute to him a sharp wit and a vivid sense of humor.

The quasi-historical book of 2 Maccabees includes a vision of Jeremiah appearing to Onias III, the last righteous high priest before politics in Jerusalem totally corrupted the office. Onias purportedly saw Jeremiah as "a man . . . distinguished by his gray hair and dignity and of marvelous majesty and authority" (2 Maccabees 15:13). Onias described him as "a man who loves the brothers and prays much for the people and the holy city" and who gave Judas Maccabeus a golden sword from God with which to defeat the foreign armies that would occupy Jerusalem (15:14–16). No doubt, Judas's success made Jeremiah yet more popular in the mind of devout Judeans during the time between the testaments.

JEREMIAH

Jesus, the Disciples, and Josephus

The respect that the Judeans held for Jeremiah perhaps explains why Jesus' disciples compared Jesus to the prophet. When Jesus asked, "Who do people say that the Son of Man is?" the disciples replied, "Some say John the Baptist, others say Elijah, and others Jeremiah or one of the prophets" (Matthew 16:13–14). The evangelist Matthew took special interest in Jeremiah, pointing out how his prophecies anticipated the suffering of the children of Bethlehem (Matthew 2:16–18) and Judas's betrayal (27:9–10). Jeremiah 31, including his prophecy of the new covenant, is one of the most popularly referenced passages in the New Testament. It fact, it is the reason we call the latter testament by that name. (The words *covenant* and *testament* are often used interchangeably.)

The early Jewish historian Josephus likewise held Jeremiah in high regard. In books 10 and 11 of his *Antiquities of the Jews*, Josephus refers to Jeremiah frequently for historical information and for interpretation of events, more often than any other Old Testament prophetic book. (Josephus's interest in the prophets may be a result of his training as a Pharisee, in contrast with the Alexandrian Jew Philo, who pays little attention to the prophetic books in his writings, perhaps due to Sadducean views.)

JESUS

Prophet of the End Times

© iStockphoto.com

Jeremiah also naturally receives significant treatment in *The Lives of the Prophets*, a first-century overview of Old Testament prophets, including material from the Bible and other accounts. For example, the book describes how Jeremiah preserved the ark of the covenant by hiding it in the wilderness, as well as Jeremiah's life and death in Egypt. Jeremiah's description of the Rechabites in Jeremiah 35 inspired *The History of the Rechabites*, a work that tells what happened to these mysterious nomadic residents of Israel who are reported to have settled on an island paradise.

After the destruction of Jerusalem and the temple in 70 AD, a number of Jewish and Christian writers used the personages of Jeremiah and Baruch to express their sorrows, since Jeremiah's prophecies had so eloquently described the first destruction of the temple and the city by the Babylonians in 587 BC. These writers also attributed visions to Jeremiah and Baruch in which they saw the end of time (2 Baruch), levels of heaven (3 Baruch), and the resurrection of the dead (4 Baruch, also known as "Things Omitted from the Prophet Jeremiah" [*Paraleipomena Jeremiou*]).

Jeremiah's Legacy and You

Jeremiah's important role in the life of Israel and in the Church should inspire you to read this suffering prophet. Perhaps think of his work as written in a minor key, solemn but sweet, describing the genuine and ongoing struggles God's people experience in this life. Recognize also that alongside his dark prophecies of God's sure judgment, Jeremiah includes the dazzling light of the promised return and the new covenant in Christ Jesus, our Savior.

The generations after Jeremiah turned to him for help in repentance, comfort in the present, and joyful hope for the future. Experience revealed that God spoke truly through Jeremiah: he said the Judeans would return in seventy years and, God be praised, they did! Now we, like Jeremiah, long for the new hour of return, the new covenant promise of Christ's return to deliver us from this dark Babylon to the light of His nearer presence.

© B-C-Designs / iStockphoto.com

Jeremiah tells us that the Lord does not willingly afflict or grieve the children of men (Lamentations 3:33). Yet, we know from other passages of Scripture that the Lord does indeed set out to discipline His people (e.g., 3:32). So what does the prophet mean? Simply that God does not ultimately wish to cause us affliction and grief. They are not the end for which He created us, since He made us "to the praise of His glory" (Ephesians 1:12).

When we experience afflictions, God's purposes are hidden from us, whether they are to humble us in repentance, as Jeremiah describes here, or are afflictions as a contest through which the heavenly Father obtains victory over sin, death, and the power of the devil as He did in the afflictions of Christ.

The Lord's Abundant Love

Three Steps in Humility

In Lamentations 3:28–30, we see the Lord leading someone into deeper humility. First, the sufferer sits alone in silence, brought down by his burden. Accepting silence in suffering is something we find difficult to do. We are born to cry out when we feel pain—from our first cry at the smack of the doctor's hand that sets us breathing as newborns, to our last gasps at life's end, instinct demands that we call for help. The sufferer here learns to suppress this instinct until only silence passes his lips as he dies to pain and to sin.

Second, Jeremiah writes that the sufferer should not only be silent but also "put his mouth in the dust" (3:29). Although this sounds like a metaphor, it likely refers to a posture of worship in which one lowers one's face to the earth in humility before God until one's breath stirs up the dust, filling one's mouth with grit.

Third and finally, Jeremiah describes the humiliating strikes of one's foe. Again, the mouth is the target of the prophet's teaching—silent, choked with dust, and now ringing out in pain. The sound of that slap fills the ears, along with insults. In silence, the sufferer speaks no evil. With his face to the dust, he sees no evil. The slaps and insults fill his ears; they fill the whole person who is hollowed out by suffering. There is nothing left of him, for he is filled with another's words and becomes a vessel cleansed of selfishness.

The Lord Will Have Compassion

Jeremiah's comments here feel unbearable, and they would be if not for the three verses that follow. He introduces these verses with the word "for" to show that the pains of humility lead to God's higher purposes. First, the prophet notes the limits God sets upon affliction. They may feel long and unbearable to us, but, Jeremiah tells us, they are not "forever." If there are three steps to humility, as the prophet described above, the first step toward God's higher purpose is to see that the suffering is not forever. Lifting our faces from the dust, our eyes look to the heavens. Eternity for God's people is bliss (Revelation 7:15–17). If suffering should rob us of life here, at the very least we know that there is a new life to come.

Second, the Lord "will have compassion" (3:32). Even as the Lord humbles us, our suffering moves Him the way a parent feels compassion when disciplining a child. The Hebrew word for "compassion" here likely comes from the word for "womb," as though He now lifts us from the dust with motherly love. Yet, this act of God is "steadfast love," or one might translate it as "loyalty, faithfulness." He grips us now and will not let us go. His abundant love fills us to overflowing, driving out the insults. His firm, gentle hand turns away the blows.

Finally, we see clearly that He does not willingly afflict or grieve His children (3:33). Cleared of insults, raised from the dust, we stand in this confidence. With His blessing, we may even see why all that trouble was necessary. We may see His will or, if not, trust Him to accomplish it through us. The vessel hollowed out by humility now overflows with the abundance of God's steadfast love and can dispense His purposes.

Call on the Lord

The children of God will experience affliction in this life, sometimes for their sins and at other times from injustice (Acts 14:22). In view of this, prepare your heart through daily repentance and appeals to God's compassion. Call upon the abundance of His steadfast love. Entrust yourself to His good and gracious will as Jeremiah describes it here at the heart of lament.

As you pray, look to the Lord Jesus, who bore our sins in silence, was laid in the dust, and was buried in our insults in order to redeem us from sin. When He rose again, He left all of that behind in the grave so that we may die to sin and live to God. In Christ, we shout praise to the Lord, bow our heads in sincerity, and are filled with His life-giving Spirit. How abundant is His steadfast love!

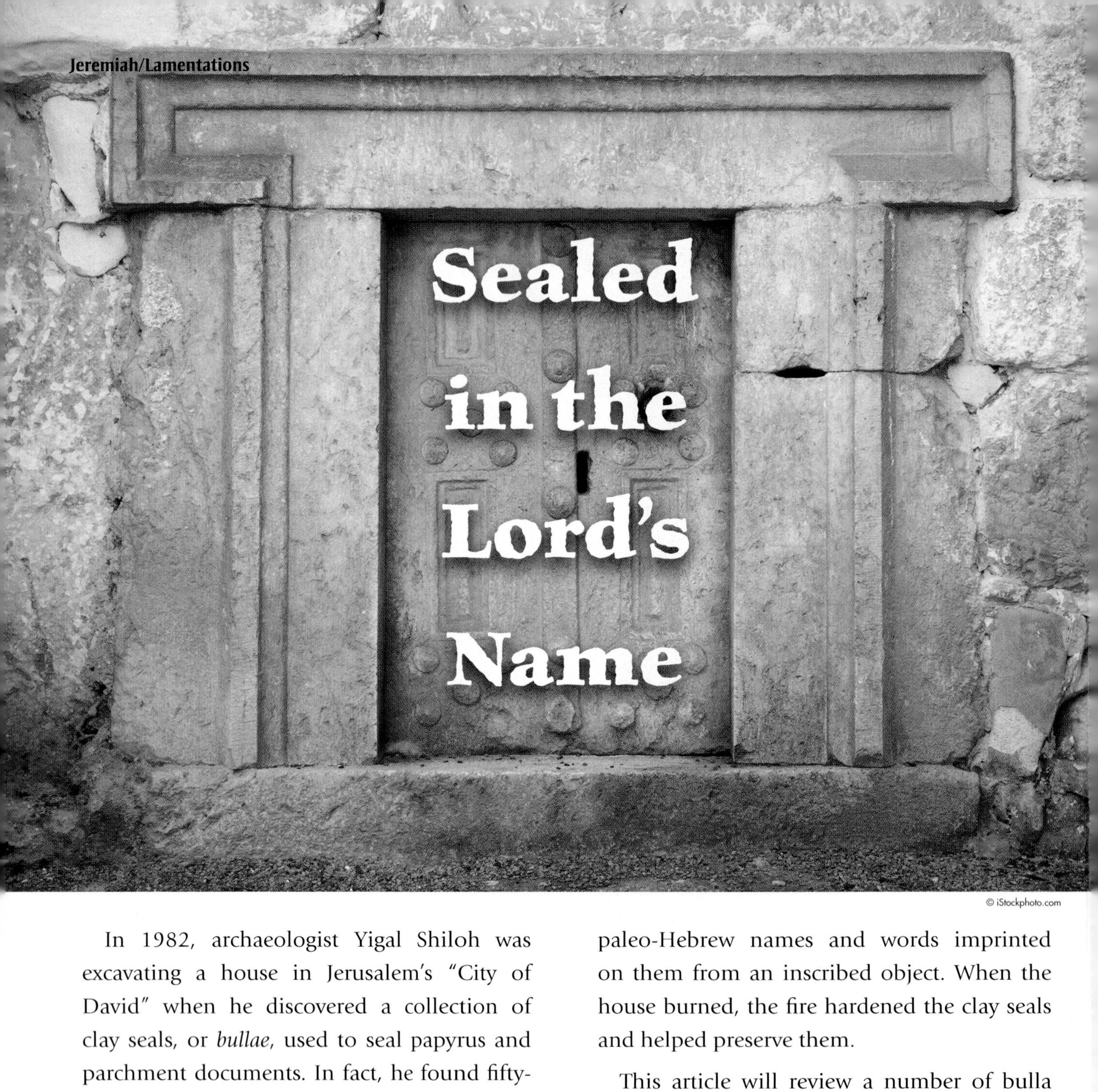

Sealed in the Lord's Name

In 1982, archaeologist Yigal Shiloh was excavating a house in Jerusalem's "City of David" when he discovered a collection of clay seals, or *bullae*, used to seal papyrus and parchment documents. In fact, he found fifty-one such seals in the ruins of a single house. This house became known as the "House of the Bullae"; it likely burned when the Babylonians destroyed the city and the temple in 587 BC. The seals had been made of soft clay, with paleo-Hebrew names and words imprinted on them from an inscribed object. When the house burned, the fire hardened the clay seals and helped preserve them.

This article will review a number of bulla seals that include the names of persons in the Book of Jeremiah. They are presented in alphabetical order. The article will also describe a unique set of inscriptions that proclaim the name of the Lord.

Baalis

This first bulla was discovered at an Ammonite city east of the Jordan River. It says, "Belonging to Milkomur servant of Baalis." Jeremiah 40:13–14 refers to this Baalis, who was an Ammonite king. Jeremiah records that Baalis sent an assassin named Ishmael to kill Gedaliah, the governor appointed by the Babylonians (see "House of Shaphan"). Ishmael succeeded in killing Gedaliah and then slipped back to Ammon (41:10). The name Baalis comes from the Canaanite god Baal.

Baruch and Neriah

The next bulla we will examine is one of hundreds discovered around Israel. It has the words "Berekyahu son of Neriyahu the scribe." The *yahu* part of the names comes from the Lord's Old Testament name, Yahweh. In English translations, *yahu* is typically represented as an "-iah" ending for names. The text of this bulla is very similar to the wording "Baruch the son of Neriah" in Jeremiah 32:12; 36:4; and numerous other passages from the prophet. Baruch was a shortened form of Berekyahu.

Neriyahu and Neriah are the same name, with a spelling variant. Although these names would be common in ancient Israel, the fact that Jeremiah's friend was a scribe and that the seal most likely belonged to a scribe point to the biblical Baruch as owner of this very seal. The name Baruch means "blessed," and the longer form on the seal would mean "blessed of Yahweh."

Gemariah

The next bulla was found in the House of the Bullae. It has the name "Gemaryahu son of Shaphan" on it. This text is exactly the same as "Gemariah the son of Shaphan" in the Hebrew of Jeremiah 36:10. Most likely, this is the personal seal of this biblical person!

As Jeremiah records, Gemariah's father was a scribe or secretary. Gemariah had a chamber-office at the temple, where Jeremiah's scribe, Baruch, publicly read a scroll of Jeremiah (ch. 36). When King Jehoiakim heard Jeremiah's message, he famously cut away the scroll piece by piece and burned it. Gemariah was among those who "urged the king not to burn the scroll" (v. 25), showing himself to be a respecter of Jeremiah. Gemariah's name means "Yahweh has brought to pass."

The House of Shaphan

The descendants of Shaphan, who likely served as royal secretary during King Josiah's reform (2 Kings 22:3–20), were on friendly terms with Jeremiah. The following diagram identifies members of Shaphan's family who are mentioned in the Book of Jeremiah, encompassing three generations of Judean officials from the time of Josiah's restoration of the temple (ca. 633 BC) to the governorship of Gedaliah (587 BC) after the Babylonian conquest.

House of Shaphan

Shaphan (Jer 26:24; 39:14)

- Ahikam (Jer 26:24; 39:14)
  - Gedaliah (Jer 39:14; 40:5)
- Elasah (Jer 29:3)
- Gemariah (Jer 36:10–11)
  - Micaiah (Jer 36:11)

Ishmael

A seal discovered in Israel says, "Belonging to Ishmael, the king's son." The name Ishmael is widely known from the time of Jeremiah, so it is unclear whether this Ishmael was the same as the one mentioned in Jeremiah 40:8 who killed governor Gedaliah. "King's son" may be the title of an official assigned to the royal household. This is worth comparing with Jeremiah's note that Ishmael was associated with "the royal family, [and] one of the chief officers of the king" (41:1).

Jerahmeel

Another seal discovered in Israel says, "Belonging to Jerahmeel the king's son," comparable with Jeremiah 36:26, "Jerahmeel the king's son," whom King Jehoiakim commanded to arrest Jeremiah and Baruch. Jerahmeel may have been King Jehoiakim's son or an official for the royal household.

The Lord Bless You

In contrast with Jeremiah's limited mentions of scribes and officials whose names appear on ancient seals, one set of seals has a name that appears 758 times in Jeremiah: the name of the Lord, Yahweh. (This figure does not include the many times Yahweh appears in names with the "-iah" ending.) In fact, the Lord's name appears far more times than the name of the prophet himself (Jeremiah's name occurs 122 times in his writings). How fitting, for ultimately Jeremiah's purpose and prophecies were to proclaim the name of the Lord and His salvation.

These unique inscriptions, which were found near Jerusalem and date from the mid-seventh to the early sixth century BC, do just that. They are little silver scrolls that were perhaps worn on necklaces. They contain the following text, known as the Aaronic Benediction:

The LORD bless you and keep you; the LORD make His face to shine upon you and be gracious to you; the LORD lift up His countenance upon you and give you peace. (Numbers 6:24–26)

Some enterprising silversmith created these tiny wonders, which contain the earliest known texts of the Bible that archaeologists have yet uncovered. Through this benediction, which is still treasured by believers today and commonly heard at the close of Christian worship services, the Lord places His name upon us to bless us and claim us as His beloved people so that He may prosper us in His way. You are sealed in the Lord's name! As you study Jeremiah, take this blessing to heart and pray with the prophet:

Blessed is the man who trusts in the LORD, whose trust is the LORD. He is like a tree planted by water, that sends out its roots by the stream, and does not fear when heat comes, for its leaves remain green, and is not anxious in the year of drought, for it does not cease to bear fruit. (Jeremiah 17:7–8)